I0759462

AMEN AND AMEN

A Timeless Collection
of Prayers and Hymns
for Life's Journey

BroadStreet Publishing® Group, LLC
Savage, Minnesota, USA
BroadStreetPublishing.com

Amen and Amen:
A Timeless Collection of Prayers and Hymns for Life's Journey

9781424570522 (faux leather)
9781424570539 (ebook)

Cover and interior by Garborg Design Works | garborgdesign.com

Printed in China

25 26 27 28 29 5 4 3 2 1

CONTENTS

INTRODUCTION

The Power of Written Prayers

Written prayers can stretch us, encourage us to pray in ways that are helpful for our faith…and teach us how to pray.

Scott Carr, Jr.

The prayer of a righteous person is powerful and effective.

James 5:16 NIV

Some of us were brought up with written prayers, and we take comfort in them. Others were brought up with impromptu or conversational prayer and may consider it "cheating" to pray someone else's prayer. You may have even heard some people claim that reciting written prayers is a poor spiritual practice. Yet there are many good reasons for written prayers.

When coming before the Lord, we may not be sure what to say. This is especially the case for new believers. I remember well the sense of dread I used to feel when asked to pray for our small group. (*Dread* is too weak a word. *Terror* is more accurate!) I wish I'd been asked to *read* a prayer out loud instead of praying impromptu.

The words of others can impart confidence as well as structure. We benefit from others' efforts—the fruit of their own struggles to express their thoughts to God in prayer. Moreover, having a template or model before us—whether we speak these prayers verbatim or simply begin with these words and expand on them thoughtfully as we pray—may keep us from rambling.

Further, a strong rationale for written or memorized prayers—such as the Psalms or the Lord's Prayer (discussed in the next chapter)—is their ubiquitous presence in the Bible. In Scripture we find not only structured prayers but also structured times: hours of prayer, days of fasting, and annual festivals. Intentional times help us to maintain our awareness of God's presence throughout the day.

Our modern world, with its countless distractions and conflicting obligations, can easily hinder our devotional life. When our schedules are full and our minds are fatigued, it's easy to let prayer slip. Without practical help from a friend, we may go through an entire day without praying at all. Accordingly, *Amen and Amen: A Timeless Collection of Prayers and Hymns for Life's Journey* offers a wide selection of prayers: formal and informal, ancient and modern, historic, scriptural, intercessory, and hymnic.

Each chapter centers on a specific theme or occasion, such as intercession, and opens with a curation of prayers. Prayers with footnotes indicate authorship, and those without footnotes are my own. An image of a harp appears after each chapter's selection of prayers, serving as a visual pause and guiding you into the chapter's accompanying hymns. Lastly, many of the selections have been edited, abbreviated, or updated for readability, and deity pronoun capitalization has been retained where original.

If you're like me, you will benefit greatly from having these prayers and hymns at your fingertips.

Douglas Jacoby

Edinburgh, Scotland

CHAPTER 1

THE LORD'S PRAYER

"This, then, is how you should pray."

MATTHEW 6:9 NIV

Jesus says, pray because you have a Father,
not because it quietens you—
and give Him time to answer.

OSWALD CHAMBERS (1874–1917)

"Our Father, who art in heaven..." I was brought up saying this prayer. Many of you were too. And I still pray this prayer nearly every day. It is certainly one of the best-known prayers in the world.

Yet Jesus wasn't sharing *his* prayer with us. It isn't a prayer for himself but for us. He was telling us how *we* should pray. After all, Jesus didn't pray for forgiveness for his own trespasses because he had none. We are to pray "Our Father"—Jesus prayed "My Father." A quick look at the context of the Lord's Prayer is in order, so let's move to the Sermon on the Mount.

> When you pray, you must not be like the hypocrites. For they love to stand and pray in the synagogues and at the street corners, that they may be seen by others. Truly, I say to you, they have received their reward. But when you pray, go into your room and shut the door and pray to your Father who is in secret. And your Father who sees in secret will reward you.
>
> And when you pray, do not heap up empty phrases as the Gentiles do, for they think that they will be heard for their many words. Do not be like them, for your Father knows what you need before you ask him. (Matthew 6:5–8 ESV)

The Lord's Prayer appears right in the middle of the Sermon on the Mount, which is a compendium of Jesus' central teachings. He urged us not to pray like the hypocrites (for attention), but to be modest, even to the point of concealing our prayers from others (vv. 5–6). The point is to cultivate the inner spiritual life.

Jesus also warned us not to mistake length for depth. Usually shorter is better (v. 7). There's no need to bring a list of our needs before the Father, as he already knows them. This is not to say that it's wrong to pray for specific things, but the Lord is already fully aware of those needs (vv. 25–34). We should focus, rather, on the bigger picture of the kingdom of God and the crucial work of growing in character to be more like Christ. Jesus told us to pray like this:

> "Our Father in heaven,
> hallowed be your name.
> Your kingdom come,
> your will be done,
> on earth as it is in heaven.
> Give us this day our daily bread,
> and forgive us our debts,
> as we also have forgiven our debtors.
> And lead us not into temptation,
> but deliver us from evil."
> (Matthew 6:9–13 ESV)

Yes, an extra sentence was added to the prayer, probably in the second century, and it has become traditional (did you miss it?), but the prayer ends here.[1] What do we notice about this prayer?

---

1 The common addition, "For yours is the kingdom and the power and the glory, forever and ever. Amen," is not found in the earliest New Testament manuscripts, neither in Matthew 6 nor Luke 11. However, the message is not unbiblical and can be included when reciting the Lord's Prayer.

- The prayer is brief and crisp—no fluff or unnecessary words. It can be recited easily and quickly. The Bible does not require us to append "in Jesus' name" to a prayer to validate it—a strong tradition without biblical support. Even *Amen* is optional![2]

- The word *our* suggests that this prayer is to be uttered not only privately but also communally.

- Jesus directed us to pray to the Father.[3] Occasionally, Christians pray to the Spirit or to Jesus himself, but Jesus encouraged prayer directly to God the Father (John 16:23). And if God is our Father, then his children are all brothers and sisters—family.

- God's name is to be "hallowed" (an archaic word meaning *sanctified* or *holy*). He is honored when we submit our lives to his sovereign care.

- Biblically speaking, God's kingdom has *always* been here, but it comes more intensively in the person of Jesus, with the outpouring of the

---

2 The Bible does not require us to bow our head or close our eyes either. In ancient artwork, in fact, Christian figures look up, not down.

3 In the Old Testament, God is portrayed as a father only 15 times, compared with some 170 times in the Gospels alone.

Spirit, and (most fully) at the end of the world.[4] "Your kingdom come" parallels "Your will be done." As the will of the Father is carried out, the kingdom spreads.

- We are to ask for daily bread, not a daily banquet. Like sensible Agur, we are to seek neither luxury nor poverty (Proverbs 30:7–9). Modesty applies both to dress and to lifestyle.
- We are to forgive others just as we have been unworthy recipients of God's grace. Matthew 6:14–15 and 18:21–35 link this with our salvation.
- We are to aim to live righteously by avoiding evil.
- It's memorable—easy to memorize and recall.

This "model prayer" isn't a prayer list but a prayer that brings our will into alignment with God's. That's why we repeat it, as our Lord instructed.

The nearly two hundred selections that follow may serve as models for us to expand on with our own words. Like the Lord's Prayer, they may also be read aloud or silently, precisely as they are written.

---

4 See Psalm 103:19; Luke 17:20–21; Acts 2:30–34; 1 Corinthians 15:24–28.

Morning Prayer

This is the day that the Lord has made;
let us rejoice and be glad in it.

Psalm 118:24 ESV

A soul without prayer is like lungs without air.

Anonymous

Do not have your concert first, and then tune your instrument afterwards. Begin the day with the Word of God and prayer, and get first of all into harmony with Him.

Hudson Taylor (1832–1905)

Strength for Today[5]

Father, this morning I thank you for the grace to desire to be with you now.

With this new day ahead of me, I pray that I may be filled with your presence, and that my faith, hope, love, and joy in you may be renewed.

Help me to renew, too, my longing for others to know you better and be closer to you.

With your steadfast love, you have been so kind to me, patient with me, and supportive of me. Let this awareness inspire me to love my friends, brothers, and sisters. Help me to be an encouragement to the discouraged—a help to bear their burdens and limitations and to lighten their loads. Keep me from words and actions that might hurt and destroy.

Keep me from making hasty conclusions and judgments about others, knowing well that we are all at different stages of growth, with different family backgrounds, values, and cultures, and that you are dealing with us in different ways.

For this, Father, I need your continued guidance and strength. Amen.

---

5 *Presence* (St Pauls Publications, 1991), 130–35.

Wesley's Prayer[6]

O Lord God Almighty, father of angels and men, we praise and bless your holy name for all your goodness and lovingkindness to humanity. We bless you for our creation, preservation, and for your unceasing generosity to us throughout our lives. But above all, we bless you for your great love in the redemption of the world by our Lord Jesus Christ. We bless you for bringing us safe to the beginning of a new day.

Grant that this day we fall into no sin, neither run into any kind of danger. Keep us, we pray, from all things hurtful to body or soul, and grant us your pardon and peace, so that being cleansed from all our sins, we might serve you with quiet hearts and minds and continue in the same until our life's end, through Jesus Christ our Savior and Redeemer. Amen.

Quiet My Mind

Father, forgive my excuses for neglecting daily prayer and show me again that deep satisfaction in life is found in a deep, abiding communion with you beginning each morning. Slow down my heart and quiet my mind that I may simply enjoy you for many moments throughout this day.

6 John Wesley (1703–1791).

Into Your Hands[7]

I thank you, my Heavenly Father, through Jesus Christ, your dear Son, that you have kept me this night from all harm and danger, and I pray that you will also keep me this day from sin and every evil, that all my doings and life may please you. For into your hands I commend myself—my body and soul and all things. Let your holy angels be with me, that the evil foe may have no power over me. Amen.

A New Day[8]

Lord God, almighty and everlasting Father, you have brought us in safety to this new day: preserve us with your mighty power, that we may not fall into sin nor be overcome by adversity. In all we do, direct us to the fulfilling of your purpose, through Jesus Christ our Lord. Amen.

The Privilege of Prayer[9]

Dear Lord, I thank you for having especially called me to pray every day. With the busy schedule I keep, I know that sometimes I take you for granted. But now, I truly wish to devote to you this time because I love you and need you in my life. Thank you for granting me the privilege of spending this time with you.

---

7 Martin Luther (1483–1546).

8 *Book of Common Prayer* (1552).

9 *Presence,* 123–124. Adapted.

As I Rise[10]

As I rise from sleep, I thank you, O Holy Trinity, for through your great goodness and patience, you were not angered with me, an idler and sinner, nor have you destroyed me in my sins but have shown your usual love for men. And when I was prostrate in despair, you have raised me to keep the morning watch and glorify your power. And now enlighten my mind's eye and open my mouth to study your words and understand your commandments and do your will and sing to you in heartfelt adoration and praise your most holy name of Father, Son, and Holy Spirit, now and ever and to the ages of ages. Amen.

Morning Needs[11]

O God, the author of all good,
I come to you for the grace this day will require...
I step out into a wicked world and know that without you, I can do nothing—
  that everything with which I shall be concerned,
  however harmless in itself,
  may prove an occasion of sin or folly, unless I am kept by your power. …
Preserve my understanding from the cunning of error,

---

10 Martin Luther (1483–1546).

11 Arthur G. Bennett, *The Valley of Vision* (Banner of Truth, 1975), 118. Adapted.

my affections from love of idols,
my character from stain of vice,
my profession from every form of evil.
May I engage in nothing in which I cannot implore your blessing and into which I cannot invite your inspection...
Teach me how to use the world and not abuse it,
to improve my talents, to redeem my time,
to walk in wisdom toward those without and in kindness to those within the world,
to do good to all men and especially to my fellow Christians.
And to you be the glory.

Morning Dedication[12]

Almighty God,
As I cross the threshold of this day,
I commit myself—soul, body, affairs, and friends—to your care.
Watch over, keep, guide, direct, sanctify, and bless me.
Incline my heart to your ways.
Mold me wholly into the image of Jesus, as a potter forms clay.
May my lips be a well-tuned harp to sound your praise.
Let those around me see me living by your Spirit,
trampling the world underfoot,

12 Bennett, *Valley of Vision*, 119. Adapted.

unconformed to lying vanities,
transformed by a renewed mind,
clad in the entire armor of God,
shining as a never-dimmed light,
showing holiness in all my doings.
Let no evil this day soil my thoughts, words, and hands.
May I travel miry paths with a life pure from spot or stain...
Let my affection be in heaven,
and my love soar upward in flames of fire:
my gaze fixed on unseen things,
my eyes open to the emptiness, fragility,
mockery of earth and its vanities.
May I view all things in the mirror of eternity,
waiting for the coming of my Lord,
listening for the last trumpet call,
hastening unto the new heaven and earth...
May I speak each word as if it were my last word
and walk each step as if it were my final one.
If my life should end today, let this be my best day.

Address God with My Heart[13]

Give me grace, Almighty Father, to pray as to deserve to be heard and to address you with my

13 Jane Austen (1775–1817), "On Each Return of the Night," janeausten.co.uk. Adapted.

heart as well as my lips. You are everywhere present; from you no secret can be hidden. May the knowledge of this teach me to fix my thoughts on you with reverence and devotion, that I may not pray in vain.

May I now, and on each return of morning, consider how I will spend the day ahead: What thoughts will prevail in my mind? What words will I speak? Will my actions reflect your will or my own? How far can I acquit myself of evil and live in the goodness and beauty of my Lord Christ?

Will I think irreverently of you? Will I disobey your commandments? Will I neglect and make excuses for any known duty, and will I knowingly give pain to any human being? Incline me to ask my heart these questions, O God, throughout the day, to save me from deceiving myself by pride or vanity.

And give me always a thankful sense of the blessings in which I live and the many comforts of my lot, that I may not deserve to lose them by discontent or indifference. Hear me, almighty God, for the sake of he who has redeemed me and taught me thus to pray. Amen.

Prayer upon Rising from Sleep[14]

My God, Father, and Savior, since you have been pleased to give me the grace to come through the night to the present day, now grant that I may employ it entirely in your service, so that all my works may be to the glory of your name and the edification of my neighbors.

As you have been pleased to make your sun shine upon the earth to give us bodily light, grant the light of your Spirit to illumine my understanding and my heart. And because it means nothing to begin well if one does not persevere, I ask that you would continue to increase your grace in me until you have led me into full communion with your Son, Jesus Christ our Lord, who is the true Sun of our souls, shining day and night, eternally and without end. Hear me, merciful Father, by our Lord Jesus Christ.

Grace for Today[15]

Lord, give me the grace for today.
Before me, the day looms with great possibilities and even greater challenges.

---

14 John Calvin (1509–1564), *Catechism of the Church of Geneva*, adapted by Tim Keller in *John Calvin [1509–1564] and Henry Beveridge, Vol. 2* (Logos Research Systems, Inc., 2009), 98–99.

15 Julie Dortch Cragon, "Morning Prayers," Franciscan Media, September 14, 2020, franciscanmedia.org.

I put them all in your hands.
Order my day, and order my life.
Help me to embrace every challenge,
to be open to all you have to give,
and to see all as opportunity—
one moment at a time, one person at a time,
and one gift at a time.
Help me to breathe in your Spirit
and to exhale any fear
that may cause me to question and to worry.
The world causes stress. You offer peace.
I choose you!

Patrick's Prayer[16]

Lord, be with us this day:
within us to purify us,
above us to draw us up,
beneath us to sustain us,
before us to lead us,
behind us to restrain us,
around us to protect us.

Walking with God[17]

Dear God, thank you for your great love and blessing over our lives. Thank you that your favor has no end,

16 Patrick of Ireland (c. AD 389–461).

17 Debbie McDaniel, "40 Good Night Prayers for Peaceful Rest in the Evening," Crosswalk, July 5, 2024, crosswalk.com.

but it lasts for our entire lifetime. Forgive us, for sometimes we forget that you are intimately acquainted with all of our ways, that you know what concerns us, and that you cover us, as with a shield.

We ask for your guidance so that we might walk fully in your blessing and goodness today. We ask that your face would shine on us. That you would open the right doors for our lives and for our loved ones, that you would close the wrong doors and guide us away from those we need to walk away from. Establish the work of our hands, and bring to fulfillment all that you have given us to do in these days.

We pray that, out of your goodness and love, you would make our way purposeful and our footsteps firm. Give us a heart of wisdom to hear your voice, and make us strong by your huge favor and grace. In Jesus' name. Amen.

Your Name Be Praised[18]

O God, early in the morning do I cry out to you;
help me to pray and to think only of you.
I cannot pray alone.
In me there is darkness, but with you there is light. I am lonely, but you leave me not. I am feeble in heart, but you leave me not.

18 Dietrich Bonhoeffer (1906–1945), *Prayers from Prison* (University of Michigan, 1977), 7. Adapted.

I am restless, but with you there is peace. In me there is bitterness, but with you there is patience.
Your ways are past understanding,
but you know the way for me.
O heavenly Father, I praise and thank you for the peace of the night. I praise and thank you for this new day.
I praise and thank you for all your goodness and faithfulness throughout my life.
You have granted me many blessings; now let me accept tribulation from your hand.
You will not lay on me more than I can bear.
You make all things work together for good
for your children.
Lord Jesus Christ, you were poor and in misery,
a captive and forsaken as I am.
You know all men's distress; you abide with me when all others have deserted me; you do not forget me but seek me.
You will that I should know you and turn to you.
Lord, I hear your call and follow you; help me.
Chiefly I remember all those imprisoned for their faith. Lord have mercy, restore them to liberty, and enable me so to live now that I may answer before you and before the world.
Lord, whatever this day may bring,
your name be praised.

I Arise Today[19]

I arise today through a mighty strength,
the invocation of the Trinity,
a belief in the threeness,
a confession of the oneness
of the Creator of creation.

I arise today through the strength of Christ's birth
and his baptism,
through the strength of his crucifixion
and his burial,
through the strength of his resurrection
and his ascension,
through the strength of his descent for the judgment
of doom.

I arise today through the strength of heaven,
light of the sun, splendor of fire,
speed of lightning, swiftness of the wind,
depth of the sea,
stability of the earth, and firmness of the rock.

I arise today through God's strength to pilot me,
God's might to uphold me,
God's wisdom to guide me,
God's eye to look before me,
God's ear to hear me,

19 Patrick of Ireland (c. AD 389–461). Adapted.

God's word to speak for me,
God's hand to guard me,
God's way to lie before me,
God's shield to protect me,
God's hosts to save me
from snares of the devil,
from temptations of vices,
from everyone who desires me ill,
afar and near, alone or in a multitude.

I summon today all these powers between me and evil,
against every cruel, merciless power that opposes my body and soul,
against the teaching of false prophets,
against the craft of idolaters,
against the error of heretics,
against every knowledge that corrupts man's body and soul.
Christ, shield me today so that reward may come to me in abundance.

Christ with me,
Christ before me,
Christ behind me,
Christ in me,
Christ beneath me,
Christ above me,
Christ on my right,

Christ on my left,
Christ when I lie down,
Christ when I sit down,
Christ in the heart of every man who thinks of me,
Christ in the mouth of every man who speaks of me,
Christ in the eye that sees me,
Christ in the ear that hears me.

Steadfast Love[20]

The steadfast love of the Lord never ceases;
his mercies never come to an end.
They are new every morning;
great is thy faithfulness.
"The Lord is my portion," says my soul,
"Therefore I will hope in him."

Holy, Holy, Holy[21]

Holy, holy, holy! Lord God almighty!
Early in the morning our song shall rise to Thee.
Holy, holy, holy! Merciful and mighty!
God in three persons, blessed Trinity.

20 Lamentations 3:22–24 (RSV).
21 Reginald Heber, "Holy, Holy, Holy," 1826.

Holy, holy, holy! All the saints adore Thee,
casting down their golden crowns
around the crystal sea.
Cherubim and seraphim falling down before Thee,
who wast and art and evermore shalt be.

Holy, holy, holy! Though the darkness hide Thee,
though the eye of sinful man Thy glory may not see,
only Thou art holy: there is none beside Thee,
perfect in pow'r, in love, and purity.

Holy, holy, holy! Lord God Almighty!
All Thy works shall praise Thy name in earth,
and sky, and sea.
Holy, holy, holy! Merciful and mighty!
God over all, and blest eternally.

Faithfulness[22]

Great is Thy faithfulness, O God my Father!
There is no shadow of turning with Thee.
Thou changest not, Thy compassions, they fail not;
as Thou hast been, Thou forever wilt be.

Summer and winter and springtime and harvest,
sun, moon, and stars in their courses above
join with all nature in manifold witness
to Thy great faithfulness, mercy, and love.

22 Thomas O. Chisholm, "Great Is Thy Faithfulness," 1923.

Pardon for sin and a peace that endureth,
Thy own dear presence to cheer and to guide,
strength for today and bright hope for tomorrow—
blessings are mine, with ten thousand beside!

Great is Thy faithfulness! Great is Thy faithfulness!
Morning by morning new mercies I see.
All I have needed Thy hand hath provided.
Great is Thy faithfulness, Lord, unto me!

Loving God

How precious is your steadfast love, O God!
The children of mankind take refuge
in the shadow of your wings.

Psalm 36:7 ESV

Prayer—secret, fervent, believing prayer—
lies at the root of all personal godliness.

William Carey (1761–1834)

The Whole of My Love[23]

Lord, because you have made me, I owe you the whole of my love. Because you have redeemed me, I owe you the whole of my self. Because you have promised so much, I owe you my whole being. Moreover, I owe you much more love than myself, as

23 Anselm of Canterbury (1033–1109). Adapted.

you are greater than I, for whom you gave yourself and to whom you promised yourself.

I pray you, Lord, make me taste by love what I taste by knowledge. Let me know by love what I know by understanding. I owe you more than my whole self, but I have no more, and by myself I cannot render the whole of it to you. Draw me to you, Lord, in the fullness of your love. I am wholly yours by creation; make me all yours, too, in love.

I Need You

Father, forgive me for despairing and not anticipating your help. Open my mind and heart to recognize the stirring of your presence and strength in my time of weakness and need.

Trusting You[24]

My God, let me know and love you so that I may find my happiness in you. Since I cannot fully achieve this on earth, help me to improve daily until I may do so to the full. Enable me to know you ever more on earth so that I may know you perfectly in heaven. Enable me to love you ever more on earth so that I may love you perfectly in heaven. In that way my joy may be great on earth, and perfect with you in heaven.

---

24 Augustine of Hippo (AD 354–430).

ONE DAY IN YOUR COURTS[25]

How lovely is your dwelling place, O LORD of hosts!
My soul longs, yes, faints, for the courts of the LORD;
my heart and my flesh sing for joy to the living God.
Blessed are those who dwell in your house, ever singing your praise!
Blessed are those whose strength is in you, in whose heart are the highways to Zion, as they go from strength to strength, for a day in your courts is better than a thousand elsewhere.
I would rather be a doorkeeper in the house of my God than to dwell in the tents of wickedness
for the LORD God is a sun and shield; you bestow favor and honor.
No good thing do you withhold from those who walk uprightly.
O LORD of hosts, blessed are all who trust in you!

TO KNOW YOU[26]

Lord Jesus, let me know myself, know you,
and desire nothing save only you.
Let me do everything for the sake of you.
Let me humble myself and exalt you.
Let me think nothing except you.
Let me die to myself and live in you.

---

25 Psalm 84:1–12 (ESV). Adapted.

26 Augustine of Hippo (AD 354–430). Adapted.

Let me accept whatever happens as from you.
Let me banish self and follow you.
Let me ever desire to follow you.
Let me flee from myself and take refuge in you.
Let me distrust myself and put my trust in you.
Let me be willing to obey for the sake of you.
Let me cling to nothing save only to you,
and let me be poor because of you.
Look upon me that I may love you.
Call me that I may see you and forever enjoy you.

Look upon us, O Lord, and let all the darkness of our souls vanish before the beams of your brightness.
Fill us with holy love and open to us the treasures of your wisdom.
All our desire is known to you; therefore, perfect what you have begun and what your Spirit has awakened us to ask in prayer.
We seek your face: turn your face toward us and show us your glory.
Then shall our longing be satisfied
and our peace be perfect.
Lead us, O God, from the sight of the lovely things of the world to the thought of you, their Creator, and grant that delighting in the beautiful things of your creation, we may delight in you, the first author

of beauty and the Sovereign Lord of all your works, blessed forevermore.

To Love You More Strongly[27]

Give me yourself, O my God, give yourself to me. Behold, I love you, and if my love is too weak a thing, grant me to love you more strongly. I cannot measure my love to know how much it falls short of being sufficient, but let my soul hasten to your embrace and never be turned away until it is hidden in the secret shelter of your presence. This only do I know, that it is not good for me when you are not with me—when you are only outside me. I want you in my very self. All the abundance of the world—which is not my God—is utter poverty. Amen.

The Selfless Giver[28]

Majestic Sovereign, timeless wisdom,
your kindness melts my hard, cold soul.
The one who loves me, selfless giver,
your beauty fills my dull, sad eyes.
I am yours: you made me.
I am yours: you called me.
I am yours: you saved me.
I am yours: you loved me.

27 Augustine of Hippo (AD 354–430). Adapted.
28 Teresa of Ávila (1515–1582). Adapted.

I will never leave your presence.
Give me death or give me life.
Give me sickness or give me health.
Give me honor or give me shame.
Give me weakness or give me strength.
I will have whatever you give. Amen.

Bless the Lord[29]

Bless the Lord, O my soul,
and all that is within me, bless his holy name!
Bless the Lord, O my soul,
and forget not all his benefits.
You forgive my iniquity and heal my diseases;
you redeem my life from the pit
and crown me with steadfast love and mercy.
You satisfy me with good
so that my strength is renewed like the eagle's.

The Lord works righteousness and justice for all who are oppressed.
You are merciful and gracious, slow to anger and abounding in love.
You will not always accuse, nor will you remain angry forever.
You do not deal with us as our sins deserve;
for as high as the heavens are above the earth,
so great is your steadfast love

29 Psalm 103:1–22 (ESV). Adapted.

toward those who fear you.
As far as the east is from the west,
so far do you remove our transgressions from us.
As a father shows compassion to his children,
so the Lord shows compassion
to those who fear him.
For you know our frame;
you remember that we are dust.
Our days are like grass;
we flourish like a flower of the field,
for the wind passes over it, and it is gone,
and its place is no more.
But the steadfast love of the Lord is from everlasting
to everlasting
on those who fear him, and his righteousness to
their children's children,
to those who keep his covenant and commandments.
You, O Lord, have established your throne
in the heavens,
and your kingdom rules over all.
Bless the Lord, O you his angels, his hosts,
his ministers who do his will.
Bless the Lord, all his works,
in all places of his dominion.
Bless the Lord, O my soul!

Divine Majesty[30]

Holy Father, Majesty in heaven, the True Divinity who lives in light unapproachable, may the splendor of your holiness and the wonder of your perfection shine in our hearts, penetrate our spirits, and nourish our souls today. We long to be with you, to bask in the warmth of your love, and to treasure the gift of your grace. Our heart's desire is to be in your presence always and to live a life that is an unbroken, uninterrupted prayer.

You know us like no other. You see our fears and our faults, our blind spots and our biases, our indiscretions and our imperfections, yet you set them against the impenetrable self-emptying love of Jesus, your Beloved. He stood in the gap, granted us access to your divine pardon, and ushered us into your unshakeable kingdom.

May your Holy Spirit enlighten the eyes of our hearts so that we may experience the joy of your holy depths. May he search the hidden recesses of our innermost being and purify us from everything that offends against your glory. Transform us from the inside out and clear the channels for the Spirit's fruit to flow as streams of living water from the oasis of your divine nature in us. May our lives draw others

---

30 Tyrone Marcus (Port of Spain, Trinidad), personal prayer, 2020.

to you so that they, too, may delight in your transcendent beauty and magnificence.

For the rest of our lives, Lord, teach us to live courageously and faithfully, showing mercy and walking in humility, to your honor and to your glory. In the name of Jesus and through the power and fellowship of the Holy Spirit, we offer this meditation of our heart and devotion of our soul to you, the only God, with reverence, gratitude, and awe. Amen.

Father, Hear My Prayer[31]

Father, hear my prayer;
I lift my voice to heaven.
To my God and King,
my heart and soul I bring,
knowing that it cost
your Son upon the cross.

Thank you for your grace,
your mercy rich in blessing,
the hope of heaven above,
on earth the brothers' love,
forgiveness that endures,
the blood that makes me pure.

Help me lift my cross
and follow you this day,

31 Ron Sawhill (Athens, Georgia), personal prayer, 2020.

proclaim your kingdom come,
lead men unto your Son,
until this world is won—
O Lord, lead me on.

Lead me not into temptation
but fill my heart with firm resolve
to proclaim this great salvation
and live life worthy of your call.

Father, hear my prayer:
I kneel in faith before you,
confident of grace
to finish out my race—
to wear the victor's crown.
O Lord, lead me on.
Amen.

Greater Confidence[32]

Dear heavenly Father, for most of my life I have tried to earn your love and gain your approval, and I felt that whatever I tried to do was never enough. In fact, the more I tried to get you to love me, the more I felt that I failed you miserably.

As I look back on the mission trips, ministry activities, times of prayer, and Bible studies, I see

32 "Prayer for Greater Confidence in God's Love," prayer.knowing-jesus.com. Adapted.

that I believed that I must be disappointing to you. I believed I wasn't doing as much as I ought to do. Father, it saddens me to realize what an incorrect perception I had of you and your love for all who are saved by grace through faith in Christ Jesus.

Father, forgive me for misrepresenting your Father-heart of love, and thank you for showing me that your love for me does not depend on what I can do for you but rests entirely on what the Lord Jesus did for me on the cross. I am accepted in the Beloved because I am a new creation in Christ, clothed in his righteousness and without condemnation. All because of Jesus.

Father, thank you for this liberating truth. May I never again be drawn into wrong thinking about your Father-heart of love, and may I gain greater confidence in and understanding of what my position in Christ truly means. This I ask in the precious name of my Lord Jesus Christ, who died for me that I might be free from any condemnation and receive your everlasting love. Praise his holy name.

I Need Your Love[33]

Oh, I need your love in this shadowed place;
I can't get enough of your sunshine on my face.
When it's cold and dark or I'm far from home,
you are in my heart, and I never walk alone.

And just like a tree planted by a stream,
thirsty for a drink of your love,
I can't face a day without some time to pray;
I sing this song to say I need your love.

I'm a tiny child, but when I'm with you
I will not grow tired,
'cause there's nothing you can't do.
Your love makes me strong,
though I'm small and weak,
and the whole day long you'll speak through me
when I speak.

You gave all for me, though I'd cursed your name.
On that bitter tree, Lord, you suffered for my shame.
How can I thank you? Your love paid my way.
All that I can do is live for you every day.

---

33 J. Brian Craig, "I Need Your Love," track 1 on *Be With Me, Lord*, Craig Productions, 2005. Used with permission.

The Deep, Deep Love of Jesus[34]

O the deep, deep love of Jesus,
vast, unmeasured, boundless, free,
rolling as a mighty ocean
in its fullness over me!
Underneath me, all around me,
is the current of Thy love,
leading onward, leading homeward
to Thy glorious rest above!

O the deep, deep love of Jesus,
spread His praise from shore to shore!
How He loveth, ever loveth,
changeth never, nevermore!
How He watches o'er His loved ones,
died to call them all His own;
how for them He intercedeth,
watcheth o'er them from the throne!

O the deep, deep love of Jesus,
love of every love the best!
'Tis an ocean vast of blessing,
'tis a haven sweet of rest!
O the deep, deep love of Jesus,
'tis a heaven of heavens to me;
and it lifts me up to glory
for it lifts me up to Thee!

34 Samuel Trevor Francis, "O the Deep, Deep Love of Jesus," 1875.

My Jesus, I Love Thee[35]

My Jesus, I love Thee; I know Thou art mine;
for Thee all the follies of sin I resign.
My gracious Redeemer, my Savior art Thou;
if ever I loved Thee, my Jesus, 'tis now.

I love Thee because Thou has first loved me
and purchased my pardon on Calvary's tree.
I love Thee for wearing the thorns on Thy brow;
if ever I loved Thee, my Jesus, 'tis now.

I'll love Thee in life; I will love Thee in death
and praise Thee as long as Thou lendest me breath
and say, when the death-dew lies cold on my brow,
"If ever I loved Thee, my Jesus, 'tis now."

In mansions of glory and endless delight,
I'll ever adore Thee in heaven so bright.
I'll sing with the glittering crown on my brow:
"If ever I loved Thee, my Jesus, 'tis now."

When My Love Grows Weak[36]

When my love to Christ grows weak,
when for deeper faith I seek,
then in thought I go to thee,
garden of Gethsemane!

35 William K. Featherston, "My Jesus, I Love Thee," 1864.

36 John R. Wreford, "When My Love to God [Christ] Grows Weak," 1837.

There I walk amid the shades
while the ling'ring twilight fades,
see that suff'ring, friendless One,
weeping, praying there alone.

When my love for man grows weak,
when for stronger faith I seek,
hill of Calvary, I go
to thy scenes of fear and woe.

There behold his agony,
suffered on the bitter tree;
see his anguish, see His faith:
love triumphant still in death.

Then to life I turn again,
learning all the worth of pain,
learning all the might that lies
in a full self-sacrifice.

O Increase My Love[37]

I pray, O Lord Jesus,
my love you'd increase
that I, like you, Jesus,
might offer men peace.
My soul wells with longing
for lips with your grace

37 Traian Dorz and Nicolae Moldovenau, "O Increase My Love," Romanian hymn, trans. Charles Brown, 1979.

and eyes of compassion
for each searching face.

O Sacred Head (Verses 1–4, 6)[38]

O sacred head, now wounded,
with grief and shame weighed down,
now scornfully surrounded
with thorns, thine only crown;
O sacred head, what glory,
what bliss till now was thine!
Yet, though despised and gory,
I joy to call thee mine.

What thou, my Lord, hast suffered
was all for sinners' gain;
mine, mine was the transgression
but thine the deadly pain.
Lo, here I fall, my Savior!
'Tis I deserve thy place.
Look on me with thy favor,
vouchsafe to me thy grace.

Men mock and taunt and jeer thee,
thou noble countenance,
though mighty worlds shall fear thee
and flee before thy glance.

38 Bernard of Clairvaux (1090–1153), "O Sacred Head, Now Wounded," trans. Paul Gerhardt, 1656, trans. James W. Alexander, 1829.

How art thou pale with anguish,
with sore abuse and scorn!
How doth that visage languish
that once was bright as morn!

My burden in thy passion,
Lord, thou hast borne for me,
for it was my transgression
which brought this woe on thee.
I cast me down before thee;
wrath were my rightful lot.
"Have mercy," I implore thee,
"Redeemer, spurn me not!"

What language shall I borrow
to thank thee, dearest friend,
for this thy dying sorrow,
thy pity without end?
O make me thine forever,
and should I fainting be,
Lord, let me never, never
outlive my love to thee.

CHAPTER 4

Security and Guidance

The Lord gives strength to his people;
the Lord blesses his people with peace.

Psalm 29:11 NIV

"I have told you these things, so that in me you may have peace. In this world you will have trouble. But take heart! I have overcome the world."

John 16:33 NIV

I have been driven many times upon my knees by the overwhelming conviction that I had nowhere else to go. My own wisdom and that of all about me seemed insufficient for that day.

Abraham Lincoln (1809–1865)

Is prayer your steering wheel or your spare tire?

Corrie ten Boom (1892–1983)

Security in God

Rest[39]

You have made us for yourself, O Lord,
and our heart is restless until it rests in you.

Safety[40]

Alone with none but you, my God,
I journey on my way.
What need I fear, when you are near,
O king of night and day?
More safe am I within your hand
than if a host did round me stand.

Peace[41]

You are the peace of all things calm.
You are the place to hide from harm.
You are the light that shines in dark.
You are the heart's eternal spark.
You are the door that's open wide.
You are the guest who waits inside.
You are the stranger at the door.
You are the calling of the poor.
You are my Lord and with me still.

---

39 Augustine of Hippo (AD 354–430).

40 Columba of Ireland (c. AD 521–597).

41 A prayer from Celtic oral tradition, first millennium.

You are my love; keep me from ill.
You are the light, the truth, the way.
You are my Savior this very day.

Trust[42]

You are my Maker.
You are my King.
You are my Comforter.
You are my Provider.
You are my Inspiration.
You are my Defender...
I trust you.

Care[43]

O Good Shepherd, seek me out, and bring me home to your fold again.
Deal favorably with me according to your good pleasure till I may dwell in thy house all the days of my life and praise you forever and ever with those who are there.

Protection[44]

May God the Father bless us;
may Christ take care of us;
the Holy Ghost enlighten us all the days of our life.

---

42 Kim Pullen (Orlando, Florida), personal prayer, 2020.

43 Jerome of Stridon (c. AD 347–420).

44 Æthelwold of Winchester (c. AD 908–984).

The Lord be our defender and keeper of body and soul, both now and forever, to the ages of ages.

Worthy[45]

You are worthy, our Lord and God,
to receive glory and honor and power,
for you created all things,
and by your will they existed and were created.

Worthy are you, Lamb of God, to take the scroll and to open its seals, for you were slain, and by your blood you ransomed people for God from every tribe and language and people and nation, and you have made us a kingdom and priests to our God, and we shall reign on the earth.

Divine Guidance

The Right Course[46]

Steer the ship of my life, good Lord, to your quiet harbor, where I can be safe from the storms of sin and conflict. Show me the course I should take. Renew in me the gift of discernment, so that I can always see the right direction in which I should go. And give me the strength and the courage to choose

45 Revelation 4:11; 5:9–10. Adapted.
46 Basil of Caesarea (AD 329–379).

the right course, even when the sea is rough and the waves are high, knowing that through enduring hardship and danger in your name we shall find comfort and peace.

Psalm 23[47]

The Lord is my Shepherd;
I shall not be in want.
He makes me lie down in green pastures;
he leads me beside quiet waters; he restores my soul.
He guides me in paths of righteousness for his name's sake.
Even though I walk through the valley of the shadow of death, I will fear no evil, for you are with me; your rod and your staff, they comfort me.
You prepare a table before me in the presence of my enemies.
You anoint my head with oil; my cup overflows.
Surely goodness and love will follow me all the days of my life, and I will dwell in the house of the Lord forever.

Guiding Hands[48]

May the guiding hands of God be on my shoulders,
may the presence of the Holy Spirit be on my head,

---

47 This prayer is a composite of Bible translations.

48 The Lorica of Fursa (AD 597–650).

may the sign of Christ be on my forehead,
may the voice of the Holy Spirit be in my ears,
may the smell of the Holy Spirit be in my nose,
may the sight of the company of heaven be in my eyes,
may the speech of the company of heaven
be in my mouth,
may the work of the church of God be in my hands,
may the serving of God and my neighbor
be in my feet,
may God make my heart his home,
and may I belong to God, my Father, completely.

Guided by You[49]

Lord, grant that I may always allow myself to be guided by you, always follow your plans, and perfectly accomplish your holy will.
Grant that in all things, great and small,
today and all the days of my life,
I may do whatever you require of me.
Help me respond to the slightest prompting of your grace so that I may be your trustworthy instrument for your honor.
May your will be done in time and in eternity by me, in me, and through me. Amen.

49 Teresa of Ávila (1515–1582).

The Road Ahead[50]

My Lord God, I have no idea where I am going. I do not see the road ahead of me. Nor do I really know myself, and the fact that I think I am following your will does not mean that I am actually doing so. But I believe that the desire to please you does in fact please you. And I hope I have that desire in all that I am doing. I hope that I will never do anything apart from that desire. And I know that, if I do this, you will lead me by the right road, though I may know nothing about it.

Therefore I will trust you always, though I may seem to be lost and in the shadow of death. I will not fear, for you are ever with me, and you will never leave me to face my perils alone.

Guiding Star[51]

Be, Lord Jesus, a bright flame before me,
a guiding star above me,
a smooth path below me,
a kindly shepherd behind me—
today, tonight, and forever.

---

50 Thomas Merton (1915–1968), *Thoughts in Solitude* (Farrar, Straus and Giroux, 1956), 79.

51 Columba of Ireland (AD 521–597).

Prayer for Absolute Protection[52]

Dear Almighty Father,
the enemy surrounds me; even my life is at risk.
So I look to the only place in the universe where I have absolute protection: the house of the Lord.
In the fear of God I find the wisdom that instructs me.
Even if they destroy me, my soul is safe.
I live eternally, only in you.
Eternal life begins today with Christ in me. I am fully protected by the bestowal of your Spirit and the spilling of your blood.
The enemy is crushed under your heel.
In the holiest of names—the name at which all must bow down—in the name of the Lord Jesus Christ.
Amen.

Just a Closer Walk with Thee[53]

I am weak, but Thou art strong;
Jesus, keep me from all wrong.
I'll be satisfied as long
as I walk, dear Lord, close to Thee.

52 "Prayer for Absolute Protection," prayerforanxiety.com. Adapted.
53 "Just a Closer Walk with Thee," 1942.

Through this world of toil and snares,
if I falter, Lord, who cares?
Who with me my burden shares?
None but Thee, dear Lord, none but Thee.

When my feeble life is o'er,
time for me will be no more.
Guide me gently, safely o'er
to Thy kingdom shore, to Thy shore.

Just a closer walk with Thee,
grant it, Jesus, is my plea.
Daily walking close to Thee,
let it be, dear Lord, let it be.

I Know That My Redeemer Lives[54]

I know that my Redeemer lives
and ever prays for me;
a token of His love He gives,
a pledge of liberty.

I find him lifting up my head;
He brings salvation near;
His presence makes me free indeed,
and He will soon appear.

54 Charles Wesley, "I Know That My Redeemer Lives," 1742.

He wills that I should holy be:
can I withstand His will?
The counsel of His grace in me
He surely shall fulfill.

Jesus, I hang upon Thy word:
I steadfastly believe
Thou wilt return and claim me,
Lord, and to Thyself receive.

CHAPTER 5

Hard Times and New Beginnings

The Lord is close to the brokenhearted
and saves those who are crushed in spirit.

Psalm 34:18 NIV

"On that day a fountain will be opened to the house of David and the inhabitants of Jerusalem, to cleanse them from sin and impurity."

Zechariah 13:1 NIV

It is because of the hasty and superficial conversation with God that the sense of sin is so weak and that no motives have power to help you to hate and flee from sin as you should.

A. W. Tozer (1897–1963)

True prayer is neither a mere mental exercise nor a vocal performance. It is far deeper than that—it is a spiritual transaction with the Creator of Heaven and Earth.

CHARLES SPURGEON (1834–1892)

HARD TIMES

FAITH AMIDST MISERY[55]

O Lord God, great is the misery that has come upon me; my cares would overwhelm me; I know not what to do.
O God, be gracious unto me and help me.
Grant me strength to bear what you send and let not fear rule over me.
As a loving person, take care of my loved ones.
O merciful God, forgive me all the sins I have committed against you and against my fellow men. I trust in your grace and commit my life wholly into your hands.
Do with me as seems best to you and as is best for me.
Whether I live or die, I am with you, and you are with me, my God.
Lord, I wait for your salvation and for your kingdom.

55 Dietrich Bonhoeffer (1906–1945), *Prayers from Prison* (University of Michigan, 1977). Adapted.

Lord, Open unto Me[56]

Open unto me—light for my darkness.
Open unto me—courage for my fear.
Open unto me—hope for my despair.
Open unto me—peace for my turmoil.
Open unto me—joy for my sorrow.
Open unto me—strength for my weakness.
Open unto me—wisdom for my confusion.
Open unto me—forgiveness for my sins.
Open unto me—love for my hates.
Open unto me—thyself for myself.
Lord—Lord, open unto me!
Amen.

Envying Nonbelievers[57]

Truly you are good to your people, to those who are pure in heart.
But as for me, my feet had almost stumbled; my steps had nearly slipped.
For I was envious of the arrogant when I saw the prosperity of the wicked.
Always at ease, they increase in riches.
I thought, "All in vain have I kept my heart clean and washed my hands in innocence."

---

56 Howard Thurman (1899–1981), *Meditations of the Heart* (Beacon Press, 1953), 145.

57 Psalm 73:1–28. Adapted.

But when I thought how to understand this, it seemed to me a wearisome task—until I went into the sanctuary of God.
Then I discerned their end.
Like a dream when one awakes, O Lord, when you rouse yourself.

You despise them as phantoms.
When my soul was embittered,
I was brutish and ignorant.
Nevertheless, I am continually with you;
you hold my right hand.
You guide me with your counsel, and afterward you will receive me to glory.

Whom have I in heaven but you?
And there is nothing on earth that I desire besides you.
My flesh and my heart may fail, but you, God, are the strength of my heart and my portion forever.

For behold, those who are far from you shall perish;
you put an end to everyone who is unfaithful to you.
But for me, it is good to be near God;
I have made the Lord God my refuge
so that I may tell of your works.

Depression[58]

Dear Lord, you are the one who created me
and the one who has provided for my salvation
and for my spiritual growth.
I firmly believe that you are a great God who loves
me very much and that you know where I am going
and what is good for me.
I humbly beseech you now, dear Lord, because I am
confused, struggling, and hurting in pain.
I am afraid and discouraged.
I feel lost and very depressed.
Let me feel your loving care and compassion.
Let me feel your sense of purpose
and understand your will for me in this crisis.
Lord, you are my refuge, my hope, and my
stronghold in this very difficult time of my life.
I lean on you and confidently put my trust in you,
for I know that you will not forsake me.
I pray that you will let time heal this wound
and that I will become a better person
because of your work in me in this crisis. Amen.

58 *Presence,* 68. Adapted.

In This Lonely Place[59]

Be my friend, O Lord,
in this lonely place.
You surround me with beauty,
but my friends are far away.

Fill my heart with joy.
With joy let me think of You.
May Your joy banish all
my lonely thoughts.

My thoughts go to a dark place
where Satan whispers lies,
where feelings reign
and truth is hard to discern.

Shine Your light, O God, upon me
and give me clear vision and discernment.
Sweep away this gloaming of spirit.

Dark Night of the Soul[60]

Lord, you are the God who saves me; day and night
I cry out to you.
May my prayer come before you;
turn your ear to my cry.

---

59 Lisa Sawhill (Athens, Georgia), personal prayer, 2020.

60 Psalm 88:1–18. Adapted.

I am overwhelmed with troubles, and my life draws near to death.
I am like one without strength.
I am set apart with the dead, like the slain who lie in the grave, whom you remember no more and are cut off from your care.
You have put me in the lowest pit,
in the darkest depths.
Your wrath lies heavily on me;
you have overwhelmed me with all your waves.
You have taken from me my closest friends and have made me repulsive to them.
I am confined and cannot escape;
my eyes are dim with grief.
I call to you, Lord, every day;
I spread out my hands to you.
I cry to you for help, Lord; in the morning my prayer comes before you.
Why, Lord, do you reject me and hide your face from me?
I have borne your terrors and am in despair.
Your wrath has swept over me; your terrors have destroyed me.
All day long they surround me like a flood; they have completely engulfed me.
You have taken from me friend and neighbor.
Darkness is my closest friend.

Disappointment[61]

Looking out from my hurt, it's hard to see clearly.
They say they want to be friends.
I've become slow to believe them—their words are spoken without action.
How can I get past this?
Counsel and instruct me, O Lord, for You know me.
I don't claim to be faultless, yet I cannot discern clearly, and the path to change is unclear.
Counsel and instruct me, O Lord, my God, the one who knows the confusion of my heart.
Years of feeling rejected or loved only because You command it of them have taken their toll.
I search eagerly for new relationships, a partnership with me in You, someone with whom I can be one in heart as Jonathan was with David—or, at least, where there is constancy.
Help me also to be what I desire of others.
How can I hope for what I am not giving?
Mend and repair me, Father.
Fill me with Your joy—the joy of Your fellowship, for without it, I have nothing in myself to give to others.
May I find delight in Your love, and smile as your precious child.

---

61 Lisa Sawhill (Athens, Georgia), personal prayer, 2020.

When God Feels Distant[62]

Father, I can barely lift my eyes to you. It's all I can do to cry out for help. Please extend your grace to me this day. Help me to see that you are in this and that you are with me. Help me to remember that you are not surprised or caught off guard by the events of this day.

Forgive me for my fears about this day. Forgive me for how I have complained and muttered about how hard this day has been. Forgive me for forgetting that you are with me. Forgive me for forgetting who I am because of what your Son, Jesus Christ, has done. Forgive me for failing to remember the glorious truths and riches I have because of the gospel.

Father, hear my prayer. Grant me gospel hope in the midst of this hard day. Help me to cling to your grace, your wisdom, and your strength.

New Beginnings

Renewal[63]

O Lord, you who have mercy upon all, take away from me my sins and mercifully kindle in me the fire of your Holy Spirit. Take away from me the heart of

62 Christina Fox, "A Prayer for Hard Days," iBelieve.com, February 9, 2022. Adapted.

63 Ambrose of Milan (c. AD 339–397).

stone and give me a heart of flesh—a heart to love and adore you, a heart to delight in you, to follow and to enjoy you, for Christ's sake.

My Whole Will[64]

Take, O Lord, and receive my entire liberty, my memory, my understanding, and my whole will. All that I possess you have given to me. I surrender it all to you, O Lord, to be disposed of according to your will. Give me only your love and your grace; with these I will be rich enough and will desire nothing more.

Source of All Mercy[65]

O my God! Source of all mercy!
I acknowledge your sovereign power.
While recalling the wasted years that are past, I believe that you, Lord, can in an instant turn this loss to gain.
Miserable as I am, yet I firmly believe that you can do all things.
Please restore to me the time lost, giving me your grace both now and in the future, that I may appear before you in "wedding garments."[66] Amen.

---

64 Ignatius of Loyola (1491–1556).

65 Teresa of Ávila (1515–1582).

66 Wedding garments symbolize righteousness. See Matthew 22:11–12 and Revelation 19:6–9.

Cleansing[67]

Almighty God, unto whom all hearts are open,
all desires known, and from whom no secrets are hid,
cleanse the thoughts of our hearts by the inspiration
of thy Holy Spirit that we may perfectly love thee
and worthily magnify thy holy Name.
Through Christ our Lord. Amen.

Strengthen My Hands[68]

Please, O Lord God of heaven, great and awesome God, who keeps his loving covenant with those who love him and obey his commandments, may your ear be attentive and your eyes be open to hear the prayer of your servant. I am praying to you both day and night on behalf of your servants, the followers of Jesus Christ. I confess the sins that we have committed against you. We have behaved corruptly against you, not obeying your commandments. Please, Lord, listen attentively to the prayer of your servant and to all who take pleasure in showing respect to your name. Grant your servants success today.

Hear, O our God, for we are despised by those who persecute us. Bless them that they may, one day, come to know the true God.

---

67 *Book of Common Prayer* (1552).

68 Composed from the prayers of Nehemiah in Nehemiah 1:5–13:28.

Please remember me for good, O my God, for all that I have done for this people. Please remember me for this, O my God, and do not ignore the kindness that I have done to honor your name. Please remember me, O my God, and have pity on me in keeping with your great love. Please remember me for good, O my God, and strengthen my hands for the work.

Yet I Will Rejoice[69]

O Lord, though the fig tree does not bud
and there are no grapes on the vines,
though the olive crop fails
and the fields produce no food,
though there are no sheep in the pen
and no cattle in the stalls,
yet I will rejoice in the Lord,
and I will be joyful in God my Savior.
The sovereign Lord is my strength.
He makes my feet like the feet of a deer.
He enables me to tread on the heights.

A Reset Today[70]

Lord, I long for those moments early in my faith when I felt your closeness, your joy, your energy, and

---

69 Habakkuk 3:17–19. Adapted.

70 Jennifer Waddle, "What to Do When You Need to Reset Your Life and Faith," iBelieve.com, January 3, 2017.

your zest for life. I confess that the daily grind has ground down my passion for you. I confess that I allow the cares of the world to choke out the joy of the gospel. Lord, turn my heart toward you again. Fix my eyes on you; fix my heart on you. Help me have a reset in my faith and in my life, starting today. Renew my heart; renew my life for you and your ways. Help me see the daily routines of life as moments to gracefully submit to your will. Thank you for being the Lord of my life every day.

Spirit of the Living God[71]

Spirit of the Living God, fall afresh on me.
Spirit of the Living God, fall afresh on me.
Break me, melt me, mold me, use me.
Spirit of the Living God, fall afresh on me.

Be Still, My Soul[72]

Be still, my soul, the Lord is on thy side;
bear patiently the cross of grief or pain.
Leave to thy God to order and provide;
in ev'ry change He faithful will remain.

71 Daniel Iverson, "Spirit of the Living God," (Birdwing Music, 1935).
72 Kathrina von Schlegel, "Be Still, My Soul," 1752, trans. Jane Borthwick, 1855.

Be still, my soul, thy best, thy heav'nly Friend
through thorny ways leads to a joyful end.

Be still, my soul, thy God doth undertake
to guide the future, as He has the past.
Thy hope, thy confidence let nothing shake;
all now mysterious shall be bright at last.
Be still, my soul, the waves and wind still know
His voice who ruled them while He dwelt below.

Be still, my soul, the hour is hast'ning on
when we shall be forever with the Lord.
When disappointment, grief and fear are gone;
sorrow forgot, love's purest joys restored.
Be still, my soul, when change and tears are past,
all safe and blessed we shall meet at last.

Breathe on Me, Breath of God[73]

Breathe on me, breath of God;
fill me with life anew
that I may love what Thou dost love
and do what Thou wouldst do.

Breathe on me, breath of God,
until my heart is pure,
Until with Thee I will one will:
to do and to endure.

---

73 Edwin Hatch, "Breathe on Me, Breath of God," 1878.

Breathe on me, breath of God
till I am wholly Thine—
till all this earthly part of me
glows with Thy fire divine.

Breathe on me, breath of God,
so shall I never die
but live with Thee the perfect life
of Thine eternity.

CHAPTER 6

HUMILITY AND CONFESSION

I confess my iniquity;
I am troubled by my sin.

PSALM 38:18 NIV

Prayer makes a godly man, and puts within him "the mind of Christ," the mind of humility, of self-surrender, of service, of pity, and of prayer. If we really pray, we will become more like God, or else we will quit praying.

E. M. BOUNDS (1835–1913)

The neglected heart will soon be a heart overrun with worldly thoughts; the neglected life will soon become a moral chaos; the heart that is not jealously protected by mighty intercession and sacrificial labors will before long become the abode of every evil bird and the hiding place for unsuspected corruption. The creeping wilderness will soon take over that church that trusts in its own strength and forgets to watch and pray.

A. W. TOZER (1897–1963)

HUMILITY

PURE HEART[74]

Give me a pure heart that I may see Thee,
a humble heart that I may hear Thee,
a heart of love that I may serve Thee,
a heart of faith that I may abide in Thee.

NOT BY MY OWN STRENGTH

Heavenly Father, grant me the humility to accept help from others where I am weak and teach me to live each day in gratitude for the gifts and strengths with which you alone have blessed me.

JOB[75]

I feel utterly insignificant.
How can I talk back to you?

74 Dag Hammarskjöld (1905–1961), *Markings*, trans. Leif Sjoberg and W. H. Auden (Ballantine Books, 1982), 83.

75 Job 40:4–5. Adapted.

I place my hand over my mouth.
I have spoken once, but no more—twice,
but now am at a total loss for words.

Empty Vessel[76]

Behold, Lord, an empty vessel that needs to be filled. My Lord, fill it. I am weak in faith; strengthen me. I am cold in love; warm me and make me fervent that my love may go out to my neighbor. I do not have a strong and firm faith; at times I doubt and am unable to trust you altogether. O Lord, help me. Strengthen my faith and trust in you. In you I have sealed the treasures of all I have. I am poor; you are rich and came to be merciful to the poor. I am a sinner; you are upright. With me there is an abundance of sin; in you is the fullness of righteousness. Therefore, I will remain with you of whom I can receive but to whom I may not give. Amen.

Total Weakness[77]

I will speak to my Lord—I who am but dust and ashes. If I consider myself anything more than this, behold, you stand against me, and my sins bear witness to a truth I cannot contradict. If I abase myself, however—if I humble myself to nothingness,

76 Martin Luther (1483–1546).

77 Thomas à Kempis (c. 1380–1471), *The Imitation of Christ,* Book 3, v. 8. Adapted.

if I shrink from all self-esteem and account myself as the dust that I am—your grace will favor me, your light will enshroud my heart, and all self-esteem, no matter how little, will sink in the depths of my nothingness to perish forever.

It is there you show me to myself—what I am, what I have been, and what I am coming to. I am nothing, and I did not know it. Left to myself, I am nothing but total weakness. But if you look upon me for an instant, I am at once made strong and filled with new joy. It is a great wonder that I, who of my own weight always sink to the depths, am so suddenly lifted up and so graciously embraced by you.

It is your love that does this, graciously upholding me, supporting me in so many needs, guarding me from so many grave dangers, and snatching me from evils without number. Indeed, by loving myself badly, I lost myself; by seeking only you and by truly loving you, I have found both myself and you. By that love, I have reduced myself more profoundly to nothing. For you, O sweetest Lord, deal with me above all my merits and above all that I dare to hope or ask.

May you be blessed, my God, for although I am unworthy of any benefits, your nobility and infinite goodness never cease to work good.

Convert us to you, that we may be thankful, humble, and devout, for you are our salvation, our courage, and our strength.

Lest I Become Proud of My Deeds[78]

You thunder forth your judgments over me, Lord. You shake all my bones with fear and trembling, and my soul is very much afraid. I stand in awe as I consider that the heavens are not pure in your sight. If you found wickedness in the angels and did not spare them, what will become of me? Stars have fallen from heaven, and I—I who am but dust— how can I be presumptuous? They whose deeds seemed worthy of praise have fallen into the depths, and I have seen those who ate the bread of angels delighting themselves with the husks of swine.

There is no holiness, then, if you, Lord, withdraw your hand. There is no wisdom if you cease to guide and no courage if you cease to defend. No chastity is secure if you do not guard it. Our vigilance avails nothing if your holy watchfulness does not protect us. Left to ourselves we sink and perish, but visited by you we are lifted up and live. We are truly unstable, but you make us strong. We grow lukewarm, but you inflame us. O how humbly and

---

78 Thomas à Kempis (c. 1380–1471), *The Imitation of Christ,* Book 3, v. 14. Adapted.

lowly should I consider myself! How very little should I esteem anything that seems good in me! How profoundly should I submit to your unfathomable judgments, Lord, where I find myself to be but nothing!

O immeasurable weight! O impassable sea, where I find myself to be nothing but bare nothingness! Where, then, is glory's hiding place? Where can there be any trust in my own virtue? All conceit is swallowed up in the depths of your judgments upon me.

What is all flesh in your sight? Shall the clay glory against him that formed it? How can he whose heart is truly subject to God be lifted up by conceit? The whole world will not make him proud whom truth has subjected to itself. Nor shall he who has placed all his hope in God be moved by the tongues of flatterers. For behold, even they who speak are nothing; they will pass away with the sound of their words, but the truth of the Lord remains forever.

Litany of Humility[79]

O Jesus, meek and humble of heart, hear me.
From the desire of being esteemed, deliver me, Jesus.
From the desire of being extolled,
    of being honored, of being praised,

79 Attributed to Rafael Cardinal Merry del Val (1865–1930). Adapted.

of being preferred to others,
of being consulted, of being approved,
deliver me, Jesus.
From the fear of being humiliated, deliver me, Jesus.
From the fear of being despised,
of being rebuked, of being neglected,
of being forgotten, of being ridiculed,
of being wronged, of being suspected,
of being injured, deliver me, Jesus.
That others may be esteemed more than I, Jesus,
grant me the grace to desire it.
That others may be chosen and I set aside,
that others may be praised and I unnoticed,
that others may be holier than I,
provided that I may become as holy as I should,
Jesus, grant me the grace to desire it.

Confession

The Jesus Prayer[80]

Lord Jesus Christ, Son of God,
have mercy on me, the sinner.

80 Desert Fathers (fifth century Egypt). See Luke 18:13.

In Mercy, Forgive[81]

Merciful God,
We confess that we have sinned against you
in thought, word, and deed.
We have not loved you with our whole heart and mind and strength.
We have not loved our neighbors as ourselves.

In your mercy forgive what we have been,
help us amend what we are,
and direct what we shall be
so that we might delight in your will
and walk in your ways
to the glory of your holy name. Amen.

Wash Me Thoroughly[82]

Have mercy on me, O God,
according to your steadfast love;
according to your abundant mercy
blot out my transgressions.
Wash me thoroughly from my iniquity,
and cleanse me from my sin.
For I know my transgressions,
and my sin is ever before me.
Against you, you only, have I sinned

---

81 *The Service for the Lord's Day: Supplemental Liturgical Resource 1* (Westminster Press, 1984), 48.

82 Psalm 51:1–17. Adapted.

and done what is evil in your sight.
You are blameless in your judgment.

Behold, you delight in truth in the inner being,
and you teach me wisdom in the inner heart.
Wash me, and I will be whiter than snow.
Let me hear joy and gladness.
Hide your face from my sins
and blot out all my iniquities.
Create in me a clean heart, O God,
and renew a right spirit within me.
Cast me not away from your presence
and take not your Holy Spirit from me.

Restore to me the joy of your salvation
and uphold me with a willing spirit.
Then I will teach transgressors your ways,
and sinners will return to you.
O Lord, open my lips,
and my mouth will declare your praise.
Truly, the sacrifices of God are a broken spirit;
a broken and contrite heart, O God,
you will not despise.

We Have Strayed[83]

Almighty and most merciful Father,
We have erred and strayed from thy ways

---

83 *Book of Common Prayer* (1552).

like lost sheep.
We have followed too much the devices and desires of our own hearts,
we have offended against thy holy laws,
we have left undone those things which we ought to have done,
and we have done those things which we ought not to have done.
But thou, O Lord, have mercy upon us;
spare thou those who confess their faults;
restore thou those who are penitent,
according to thy promises declared unto mankind in Christ Jesus our Lord;
and grant, O most merciful Father, for his sake, that we may hereafter live a godly, righteous, and sober life to the glory of thy holy name. Amen.

Deep in Guilt[84]

O my God, I am ashamed and blush to lift my face to you, for our iniquities have risen higher than our heads, and our guilt has mounted up to the heavens. We are deep in guilt. We seek your favor. Brighten our eyes and grant us revival.

Now, O our God, what shall we say? We have forsaken your commandments. O Lord, the God of Israel, you are just. Behold, we are before you

84 Ezra 9:6–15. Adapted.

in our guilt, and none can stand before you. Smile upon us again.

LISTEN AND ACT![85]

O great and awesome God, who keeps his covenant and mercy with those who love him and keep his commandments, I have sinned and committed iniquity. I have done wickedly and rebelled by departing from your precepts and judgments. Neither have I heeded your many reminders—through conscience, Scriptures, the wise counsel of friends, and the prompting of your Spirit.

O Lord, righteousness belongs to you, but shame to me because of my unfaithfulness against you. To you belong mercy and forgiveness, even though your people have rebelled against you. Disaster has come upon us, yet we have failed to turn to you in prayer.

O Lord, according to all your righteousness, let your anger and fury be turned away from us.

Now therefore, our God, hear the prayer of your servant, and for your sake cause your face to shine on us. O my God, incline your ear and hear; open your eyes and see our desolations. For we dare not present our supplications before you because of our righteous deeds but because of your great mercies.

---

85 Daniel 9:4–19. Adapted.

O Lord, hear! O Lord, forgive! O Lord, listen and act! Do not delay for your own sake, my God, for we are called by your name.

Weighted Down[86]

O Lord Almighty, God of our ancestors, of Abraham and Isaac and Jacob and of their righteous offspring; you who made heaven and earth with all their order, who shackled the sea by your word of command, who confined the deep and sealed it with your terrible and glorious name; at whom all things shudder and tremble before your power, for your glorious splendor cannot be borne, and the wrath of your threat to sinners is unendurable. Yet immeasurable and unsearchable is your promised mercy, for you are the Lord Most High, of great compassion, longsuffering, and very merciful, and you relent at human suffering.

O Lord, according to your great goodness, you have promised repentance and forgiveness to those who have sinned against you, and in the multitude of your mercies you have appointed repentance for sinners so that they may be saved. Therefore you, O Lord, God of the righteous, have provided repentance for me, a sinner. For the sins I have

---

86 "The Prayer of Manasseh." Though apocryphal, this prayer fits well with the story of Manasseh's repentance in 2 Chronicles 33:10–19.

committed are more in number than the sand of the sea. My transgressions are multiplied, O Lord—they are multiplied! I am not worthy to look up and see the height of heaven because of the multitude of my iniquities. I am weighted down with many an iron fetter, and I have no relief, for I have provoked your wrath and have done what is evil in your sight, setting up idols in my heart and multiplying offenses.

And now I bend the knees of my heart, imploring you for your kindness. I have sinned, O Lord, I have sinned—I admit it. I earnestly implore you: Forgive me, O Lord, forgive me! Do not destroy me along with my transgressions. Do not be angry with me forever. For you, O Lord, are the God of those who repent, and in me you will manifest your goodness. For, unworthy as I am, you will save me according to your great mercy, and I will praise you continually all the days of my life. Amen.

Out of the Depths[87]

Out of the depths I cry to you, Lord.
Lord, hear my voice; let your ears be attentive to my cry for mercy.
If you, Lord, kept a record of sins, who could stand?
But with you there is forgiveness, so that we can serve you with reverence.

87 Psalm 130:1–8. Adapted.

I wait for the LORD—my whole being waits—
and in his Word I put my hope.
I wait for the Lord more than watchmen wait
for the morning.
Let me and my fellow believers put our hope
in the LORD, for with the LORD is unfailing love
and full redemption.
He himself will redeem his people from all their sins.

AN ACT OF CONTRITION[88]

O God,
I am sorry for having offended You, and I detest all my sins: they hurt me, they hurt others, but most of all, they offend you, O my God.

In choosing to do wrong and failing to do good, I have sinned against you, who deserves the love of all my heart, soul, mind, and strength.

I firmly intend, with the help of your grace, to repent, to sin no more, and to avoid whatever leads me to sin.

Our Lord and Savior Jesus Christ suffered and died for our sins, and I want him to suffer no more.

Enable me to hate sin, flee from it, and love righteousness. Lord have mercy on me, a sinner. Then I will teach sinners your ways and make your grace and holiness known for your glory and honor. Amen.

---

88 "Act of Contrition," usccb.org. Adapted.

Out of the Slimy Pit[89]

You lifted me out of the slimy pit,
the mud, and the mire;
You set my feet on a rock
and gave me a firm place to stand.
You put a new song in my mouth:
a hymn of praise to my God.
Many will see and fear the Lord
and put their trust in him.

O God, Whose Hand[90]

O God, whose hand has spread the sky
and all its shining hosts on high,
and, painting it with fiery light,
made it so beauteous and so bright.

Illuminate our hearts within,
and cleanse our minds from stain of sin;
unburdened of our guilty load,
may we unfettered serve our God.

Grant this, O Father, ever One
with Christ, your sole-begotten Son,
whom with the Spirit we adore,
one God, both now and evermore.

---

89 Psalm 40:2–3. Adapted.

90 Gregory the Great (AD 540–604), *Cœli Deus Sanctissime, Liturgia Horarum,* trans. J. M. Neale, 1854. Adapted.

Unto Thee, O Lord[91]

Unto Thee, O Lord, do I lift up my soul.
Let none that wait on Thee be ashamed.
Remember not the sins of my youth.
Teach me Thy paths and ways, O Lord.

O my God, I trust in Thee.
Let me not be ashamed;
let not my enemies triumph over me.

Have Thine Own Way[92]

Have Thine own way, Lord! Have Thine own way!
Thou art the Potter; I am the clay.
Mold me and make me after Thy will
while I am waiting, yielded and still.

Have Thine own way, Lord! Have Thine own way!
Search me and try me, Master, today!
Whiter than snow, Lord, wash me just now
as in Thy presence humbly I bow.

Have Thine own way, Lord! Have Thine own way!
Hold o'er my being absolute sway!
Fill with Thy Spirit till all shall see
Christ only, always, living in me!

---

91 Psalm 25:1–4, 7. Adapted.

92 Adelaide Pollard, "Have Thine Own Way, Lord," 1906.

Lead Me to Calvary[93]

King of my life, I crown Thee now;
Thine shall the glory be.
Lest I forget Thy thorn-crowned brow,
lead me to Calvary.

Show me the tomb where Thou wast laid,
tenderly mourned and wept;
angels in robes of light arrayed
guarded Thee whilst Thou slept.

Let me like Mary, through the gloom,
come with a gift to Thee;
show to me now the empty tomb;
lead me to Calvary.

May I be willing, Lord, to bear
daily my cross for Thee;
even Thy cup of grief to share—
Thou hast borne all for me.

Lest I forget Gethsemane,
lest I forget Thy agony,
lest I forget Thy love for me,
lead me to Calvary.

---

93 Jennie Evelyn Hussey, "Lead Me to Calvary," 1921.

Nearer, Still Nearer[94]

Nearer, still nearer, close to Thy heart,
draw me, my Savior, so precious Thou art;
fold me, O fold me, close to Thy breast;
shelter me safe in that haven of rest.

Nearer, still nearer; nothing I bring:
naught as an off'ring to Jesus my King.
Only my sinful, now contrite heart;
grant me the cleansing Thy love doth impart.

Nearer, still nearer, Lord, to be Thine,
sin with its follies I gladly resign.
All of its pleasures, pomp, and its pride;
give me but Jesus, my Lord crucified.

Nearer, still nearer, while life shall last
till, safe in glory, my anchor is cast.
Through endless ages, ever to be
nearer, my Savior, still nearer to Thee.

94 Leila N. Morris, "Nearer, Still Nearer," 1904.

ZEAL AND CHARACTER

Zeal for your house consumes me.

PSALM 69:9 NIV

You must pray with all your might. That does not mean saying your prayers, or sitting gazing about in church or chapel with eyes wide open while someone else says them for you. It means fervent, effectual, untiring wrestling with God. You can be sure that this kind of prayer the devil and the world and your own indolent, unbelieving nature will oppose. They will pour water on this flame.

WILLIAM BOOTH (1829–1912)

A few songs with Him might change the way you sing. Forever.

MAX LUCADO (1955–)

Zeal

Set Our Hearts on Fire[95]

The night has passed,
and the day lies open before us;
let us pray with one heart and mind.
Silence is kept.
As we rejoice in the gift of this new day, so may the light of your presence, O God, set our hearts on fire with love for you, now and forever. Amen.

Hunger and Thirst for God[96]

O God of truth, grant me the happiness of heaven so that my joy may be full, in accord with your promise. In the meantime, let my mind dwell on that happiness, my tongue speak of it, my heart pine for it, my mouth pronounce it, my soul hunger for it, my flesh thirst for it, and my entire being desire it until I enter through death into the joy of my Lord forever. Amen.

A Syrian Prayer[97]

O God, who is the unsearchable abyss of peace, the ineffable sea of love, the fountain of blessings, and the bestower of affection, who sends peace to those

95 *Book of Common Prayer* (1552).
96 Augustine of Hippo (AD 354–430).
97 Syrian Clementine Liturgy, first century.

that receive it, open to us this day the sea of your love and water us with the plenteous streams from the riches of your grace. Make us children of quietness and heirs of peace. Kindle in us the fire of your love. Sow in us your fear. Strengthen our weakness by your power. Bind us closely to you and each other in one firm bond of unity for the sake of Jesus Christ. Amen.

Feed the Beggar[98]

O most kind, most loving Lord, whom I now desire to receive with devotion, you know the weakness and the necessity which I suffer, in what great evils and vices I am involved, and how often I am depressed, tempted, defiled, and troubled.

To you I come for help; to you I pray for comfort and relief. I speak to him who knows all things, to whom my whole inner life is manifest, and who alone can perfectly comfort and help me.

You know what good things I am most in need of and how poor I am in virtue. Behold, I stand before you, poor and naked, asking your grace and imploring your mercy. Feed your hungry beggar. Inflame my coldness with the fire of your love. Enlighten my blindness with the brightness of your

98 Thomas à Kempis (c. 1380–1471), *The Imitation of Christ,* Book 4, chapter 16. Adapted.

presence. Turn all earthly things to bitterness for me, all grievance and adversity to patience, and all lowly creation to contempt and oblivion. Raise my heart to you in heaven, and permit me not to wander on earth. You alone are my food and drink, my love and my joy, my sweetness and my total good.

Let your presence wholly enflame, consume, and transform me into yourself so that I may become one spirit with you by the melting power of your ardent love. Let me not go from you hungry and thirsty but deal with me mercifully. It would be no wonder if I were completely inflamed by you to die to myself since you are the fire ever burning and never dying—a love purifying the heart and enlightening the understanding.

Fire in My Soul[99]

Holy Spirit, powerful consoler, sacred bond of the Father and the Son, hope of the afflicted, descend into my heart and establish in it your loving dominion. Kindle in my tepid soul the fire of your love so that I may be wholly subject to you. We believe that when you dwell in us, you also prepare a dwelling for the Father and the Son. Deign, therefore, to come to me, consoler of abandoned souls and protector of the needy. Help the afflicted,

99 Augustine of Hippo (AD 354–430).

strengthen the weak, and support the wavering. Come and purify me. Let no evil desire take possession of me. You love the humble and resist the proud. Come to me, glory of the living and hope of the dying. Lead me by your grace that I may always be pleasing to you. Amen.

CHARACTER

COURAGE[100]

From the cowardice that shrinks from new truths, from the laziness that is content with half-truths, from the arrogance that thinks it knows all truths, dear God of truth, deliver me!

DYING TO SELF[101]

Govern everything by your wisdom, O Lord, so that my soul may always be serving you in the way you will and not as I choose. Let me die to myself so that I may serve you; let me live to you who is life itself. Amen.

---

100 "O God of Truth," ancient prayer.

101 Teresa of Ávila (1515–1582).

The Giver[102]

Great are you, O Lord! Creator, designer, planner,
and the giver and origin of all that is good.
Your goodness surrounds me:
through the delights of your creation,
through the hands of your kingdom,
through the planning of my family,
you have loved and blessed me.
Your blessings come freely.
Undeserved.

No repayment is possible.
Guard my heart from the guile of the evil one.
Let it overflow with gratitude for your grace—
expressed abundantly in numerous ways.
Let my heart be like Paul's, who worked harder
because of your grace,
or like Zacchaeus', whose heart filled with joy and
whose life changed.
Your grace was infinitely more valuable to them than
silver or gold.

Guide my heart in putting your blessings to work
that they may bless others also.
Let my hand not grasp them too tightly
in fear of losing them.

---

102 Lisa Sawhill (Athens, Georgia), personal prayer, 2020.

Let them not become more important to me
than you, the giver.

And when it is time in your eyes
for the blessings to dim
and suffering to come
(as it does to all),
let me forever praise you
and cling to you, my Maker.
Let me hold fast to you, the one who loves me.
You are the giver of grace in times of blessing,
You are the giver of grace in times of suffering.

GENEROSITY[103]

Lord, teach me to be generous,
to serve you as you deserve,
to give and not to count the cost,
to fight and not to heed the wounds,
to toil and not to seek for rest,
to labor and not to look for any reward,
save that of knowing that I do your holy will.

CONSISTENCY[104]

Let nothing disturb me;
let nothing frighten me.
All things are passing.

103 Ignatius of Loyola (1491–1556).
104 Teresa of Ávila (1515–1582).

God never changes.
Patience obtains all things.
Nothing is wanting to him who possesses God.
God alone suffices.

Wycliffe's Prayer[105]

Lord, give me grace to hold righteousness
in all things
that I may lead a clean and blessed life
and prudently flee evil
and that I may understand the treacherous
and deceitful falseness of the devil.
Make me mild, peaceable, courteous, and temperate.
And make me steadfast and strong.
Also, Lord, give Thou to me that I be quiet in words
and that I speak what is appropriate.

Strengthen Us[106]

God, our Father, we are exceedingly frail and indisposed to every virtuous and gallant undertaking. Strengthen our weakness, we beseech you, that we may do valiantly in this spiritual war; help us against our own negligence and cowardice, and defend us from the treachery of our unfaithful hearts for Jesus Christ's sake.

105 John Wycliffe (c. 1328–1384).
106 Thomas à Kempis (c. 1380–1471).

Change My Heart[107]

O Son of God, perform a miracle for me:
change my heart.
You, whose crimson blood redeems mankind,
whiten my heart.
It is you who make the sun bright
and the ice sparkle,
you who make the rivers flow and the salmon leap.

Your skilled hand makes the nut tree blossom
and the corn turn golden;
your Spirit composes the song of the birds
and the buzz of the bees.
Your creation is a million wondrous miracles,
beautiful to behold.
I ask of you just one more miracle: beautify my soul.
Amen.

Abundantly More[108]

I bow before you, Father, from whom every family in heaven and on earth is named, that according to the riches of your glory, you may grant that I be strengthened with power through your Spirit in my inner being, so that Christ may dwell in my heart through faith. I pray that, being rooted and

107 Celtic prayer (c. AD 450–700).
108 Paul's prayer in Ephesians 3:14–21. Adapted.

grounded in love, I may have strength to comprehend with all the saints what is the breadth and length and height and depth, and to know the love of Christ that surpasses knowledge, that I may be filled with all the fullness of God.

Now to you who are able to do far more abundantly than all that we ask or think, according to the power at work within us—to you be glory in the church and in Christ Jesus throughout all generations forever and ever. Amen.

The Strength to Seek You[109]

O Lord my God, I believe in you, Father, Son, and Holy Spirit. Insofar as I can—insofar as you have given me the power—I have sought you. I became weary, and I labored. O Lord my God, my sole hope, help me to believe and never to cease seeking you. Grant that I may always and ardently seek out your countenance.

Give me the strength to seek you, for you help me to find you, and you have more and more given me the hope of finding you. Here I am before you with my firmness and my infirmity. Preserve the first and heal the second. Here I am before you with my strength and my ignorance. Where you have opened the door to me, welcome me at the entrance; where

109 Augustine of Hippo (AD 354–430).

you have closed the door to me, open to my cry. Enable me to remember you, to understand you, and to love you. Amen.

AWAKE AND ALERT[110]

Almighty Lord, God of the powers and of all flesh, who lives in the highest and cares for the humble, who searches our hearts and affections, and who clearly foreknows the secrets of men; eternal and ever-living light, in whom is no change nor shadow of variation; O immortal king, receive our prayers which we offer to you from unclean lips, trusting in the multitude of your mercies.

Forgive all sins that we commit in thought, word, or deed, consciously or unconsciously, and cleanse us from all defilement of flesh and spirit. Grant us to pass the night of the whole present life with wakeful heart and sober thought, ever expecting the coming of the radiant day of the appearing of your Son, our Lord and God and Savior, Jesus Christ, when the judge of all will come with glory to render to each according to their deeds.

May we not be found fallen and idle but awake and alert for action, ready to accompany him into the joy and divine palace of his glory, where there is the ceaseless sound of those keeping festival and the

110 Basil of Caesarea (AD 330–379).

unspeakable delight of those who behold the ineffable beauty of your face. For you are the true light that enlightens and sanctifies all, and all creation sings to you throughout the ages. Amen.

Thy Grace Impart[111]

O Lord, Thy heavenly grace impart
and fix my frail, inconstant heart;
henceforth my chief desire shall be
to dedicate myself to Thee—
to Thee, my God, to Thee.

Whate'er pursuits my time employ,
one thought shall fill my heart with joy:

that silent, secret thought shall be
that all my hopes are fixed on Thee—
on Thee, my God, on Thee.

Lord of All[112]

If life is just a song, I will sing for you.
If life is just a path, I will walk for you,
Jesus, Jesus, Lord of all.

111 Jean Frederic Oberlin (1740–1826), "Thy Grace Impart," 1853.

112 Larry Jackson, "Lord of All," Discipleship Publications International, 1989. Used with permission.

Down upon the earth to set me free,
to break the chains that had a hold on me,
Jesus, Jesus, Lord of all.

Always by my side to comfort me,
always by my side to carry me,
Jesus, Jesus, Lord of all.

The world that we know will pass away;
the life that you give will forever stay,
Jesus, Jesus, Lord of all.

I'm Not Ashamed[113]

I'm not ashamed to own my Lord
or to defend his cause,
maintain the honor of his Word—
the glory of his cross.

Jesus, my God! I know his name;
his name is all my trust;
nor will he put my soul to shame
nor let my hope be lost.

Firm as his throne his promise stands,
and he can well secure
what I've committed to his hands
till the decisive hour.

113 Isaac Watts, "I'm Not Ashamed to Own the Lord," 1709.

Then will he own my worthless name
before his Father's face
and in the new Jerusalem
appoint my soul a place.

Making an Impact for Christ

For to me, to live is Christ and to die is gain.
If I am to go on living in the body,
this will mean fruitful labor for me.

PHILIPPIANS 1:21–22 NIV

Authentic transformation is possible if we are willing to do one thing, and that is to arrange our lives around the kind of practices and life Jesus led to be constantly receiving power and love from the Father.

DALLAS WILLARD (1935–2013)

Prayers lay down the track on which God's power comes. Like a mighty locomotive, his power is irresistible, yet it cannot reach us without rails.

WATCHMAN NEE (1903–1972)

An Instrument of Your Peace[114]

Lord, make me an instrument of your peace.
Where there is hatred, let me sow love;
where there is injury, pardon;
where there is doubt, faith;
where there is despair, hope;
where there is darkness, light;
where there is sadness, joy.
O divine Master, grant that I may
not so much seek to be consoled as to console,
not so much to be understood as to understand,
not so much to be loved as to love.
For it is in giving that we receive;
it is in pardoning that we are pardoned;
it is in dying that we awake to eternal life.

Overflow

Dear Lord, saturate me with the experience of the love only you can give, so that it overflows from me to all whom I encounter throughout all the days of my life.

114 Francis of Assisi (1181–1226).

Speak, Lord[115]

Father God in heaven, I pray that you would fill me with your Holy Spirit as I read your Word and bless me with wisdom, understanding, intelligence, and focus so that I would know you and make you known. Speak, Lord, for your servant is listening.

Prayer for Boldness[116]

Lord, you are God, who made heaven and earth and the sea and all that is in them, who in the Scriptures spoke of the Messiah to come and of his rejection by the authorities. They still oppose you.

In our own day, there are dark forces in play, and many are the enemies of the gospel. Now, Lord, consider their threats and empower your servants so that with all boldness we may speak your Word. Now fill us with the Spirit of Christ, that we may speak the Word with boldness.

Troubled Over the Lost[117]

Lord, I am deeply troubled, and my heart aches over the fate of those who do not know you. So many of us have family in worldly Sodom. Will you indeed sweep away the righteous with the wicked? Would

---

115 Ally Boyd (Edinburgh, Scotland), personal prayer inspired by 1 Samuel 2, 2020.

116 The Believers' Prayer for Boldness in Acts 4:24–31. Adapted.

117 Abraham's prayer in Genesis 18:23–32. Adapted.

the good be condemned along with the wicked? Far be that from you! Far be it from you to do such a thing—to assign the same judgment to the righteous as to the wicked. I know and trust that the judge of all the earth will do right.

I have dared to speak to the Lord—I who am but dust and ashes. Hear my plea. Be merciful. As Christians, we know that the good news of the gospel must reach even the Sodoms of our world. If I am to be part of the solution, I'm ready to do whatever you call me to do. Please make that clear. Thank you for your grace. May it continue to wash over the earth as more and more people turn to you.

At My Job

Dear God, thank you that I have a job. In so many countries, unemployment is dangerously high. Help me to enjoy my work even when things are dull or humdrum.

I am aware that I represent you, so help me to arrive punctually, to strive for excellence, to be respectful to all, and to serve my superiors not only when their eyes are on me but also at the other times. When I'm working from home, let me have the same standards as I would in any workplace, aiming to do my best for you, Lord.

As a follower of Christ, protect me from all involvement in shady practices. Let me speak and act honestly. Finally, let me never put the job above things that count more: my family, my integrity, and my faith.

In My Neighborhood

Thank you, Lord God, that I have a comfortable place to live even while many in our world lack comfort or housing. Here you have placed me in the midst of many who do not know you, and I know it is your will to work through me.

Please nudge me any time when I am tempted to ignore my neighbors or to be unfriendly. Help me overcome inhibitions and strike up conversations. Show me whom to invite to my home so that by my hospitality, they may feel the love of Christ. Provide many opportunities for us to open your Word. I deeply long to lead others to Christ, and for that, I need your wisdom and direction. Amen.

In My Education

Dear Lord, I am so privileged and so grateful. With so few people able to afford the time or money to attend school, I am truly blessed. Help me not to take my education for granted.

Let me have an impact during my years here. As an ambassador for Christ, lead me to open hearts. May your Spirit sensitize my conscience so that I do nothing that will repel others from the gospel message. Help me also to study hard, showing others that it is the Lord Christ I am serving. Finally, guide me so that this investment of time and mental energy pays off for future service in your kingdom. Bring glory to your name, O Lord.

Here Am I—Send Me![118]

Holy, holy, holy is the Lord of hosts;
the whole earth is full of His glory!
I am overwhelmed, shattered, terrified—
woe is me, for I am undone!
I am a person of unclean lips,
and I dwell in the midst of a people of unclean lips.
Yet my eyes have seen the King,
the Lord of hosts.

I accept the mission that you command
just as I accept the cleansing that you offer.
My iniquity is taken away; my sin is purged.
Whom shall you send?
"Here am I! Lord, send me!"

---

118 Isaiah 6:3–8. Adapted.

Thanks, Praise, and Glory[119]

Father, I thank you;
Lord, I do praise your name!
May I glorify you each night and day,
love and adore you, be the door for you
to enter others' lives and free them from sin,
grace and glory to usher in,
life of eternity, even to begin.
Father, I thank you.
Lord, I do praise your name!
May I glorify you all of my life.
May I glorify you all of my life.

Outreach[120]

Lord Jesus Christ, who didst stretch out thine arms
of love on the hard wood of the cross
that everyone might come within the reach of thy
saving embrace,
so clothe us in thy Spirit that we,
reaching forth our hands in love,
may bring those who do not know thee
to the knowledge and love of thee,
for the honor of thy name. Amen.

119 Ron Sawhill (Athens, Georgia), personal prayer, 2020.
120 *Book of Common Prayer* (1552).

Apprentice Prayer[121]

Jesus, I love you! Father, I adore you! Holy Spirit, I rely on you!

Thank you, Jesus, for your cross. Thank you, Father, for your eternal love. Thank you, Holy Spirit, for your presence and power. Holy Trinity, I praise you.

Lord Jesus, you're my teacher. I seek to live as your apprentice in all that I do today. My life is your school for teaching me. I relinquish my agenda for this day, and I submit myself to you and your kingdom purposes. In all situations, I abandon outcomes to you, praying, "Your will, your way, your time."

Dear Father, I ask you to ordain the events of this day and use them to make me more like Jesus. I ask and trust you, Sovereign Lord, that you won't let anything happen to my family or me today except that it passes through your loving hands. So no matter what problems, hardships, or injustices I face today, help me not to worry or get frustrated, but instead to relax in the yoke of your providence. Yes, today I will rejoice because I am in your eternal kingdom, you love me, and you are teaching me.

My Creator and Redeemer, I devote my whole self to you. I want to be all and only for Jesus.

---

121 Bill Gaultiere, "The Apprentice Prayer," soulshepherding.org.

Today, I love you with all my heart, all my soul, all my mind, all my strength, and all my relationships.

Today, I depend on you, Holy Spirit—not my own resources. Help me to keep in step with you. Today, I look to love others as you love me, dear God, blessing everyone I meet, even those who mistreat me. Today, I'm ready to lead people to follow you, Jesus. Amen.

Covenant Prayer[122]

I am no longer my own, but yours.
Put me to what you will;
place me with whom you will.
Put me to doing; put me to suffering.
Let me be put to work for you or set aside for you,
praised for you or criticized for you.
Let me be full; let me be empty.
Let me have all things; let me have nothing.
I freely and fully surrender all things to your glory
and service.
And now, O wonderful and holy God,
Creator, Redeemer, and Sustainer,
you are mine, and I am yours.
So be it.

---

122 John Wesley (1703–1791).

And the covenant which I have made on earth,
let it also be made in heaven. Amen.

A Faithful God[123]

O Lord, God of Israel, there is no God like you in heaven above or on earth beneath. Behold, heaven and the highest heaven cannot contain you! Through your holy covenant, you show steadfast love to your servants—to those who walk before you with all their heart. Listen to the cry and to the prayer that I, your servant, pray before you this day, and when you hear, forgive.

Likewise, when outsiders, who are not of your people, come near and pray for your name's sake (for they shall hear of your great name and your mighty acts), hear in heaven and answer their prayer, in order that all the peoples of the earth may know your name. May they come to know that you are the true God and there is no other.

Blessed are you, O Lord: not one word of all your good promises has ever failed. I long to be equally faithful in my own life. Fortify my heart, that I may be wholly true to you, O Lord our God, walking in all your statutes and keeping all your commandments.

123 Solomon's prayer in 1 Kings 8:23–61. Adapted.

Spreading Your Fragrance[124]

Dear Jesus, help us to spread your fragrance everywhere we go.
Flood our souls with your spirit and life. Penetrate and possess our whole being so utterly that our lives may be a radiance of yours. Shine through us and be so in us that every soul we come in contact with may feel your presence in our soul.

Reinvigorated and Protected[125]

Father God, I am reinvigorated in my faith, and I hunger for your love in my life. I ask that you continue to hold my hand as I walk toward your light. You have declared the purpose for my life, and as I continue to grow closer to you, please do not let go of my hand. Thank you, Lord. Amen.

Take My Life and Let It Be[126]

Take my life, and let it be consecrated, Lord, to Thee; take my moments and my days; let them flow in ceaseless praise.

---

124 John Henry Newman, *Heart Speaks to Heart: Selected Spiritual Writings*, ed. Lawrence Cunningham (New City Press, 2004), 47–48.

125 Rae, "God's Great Love," prayer request, July 21, 2014, prayer.knowing-jesus.com.

126 Frances R. Havergal, "Take My Life, and Let It Be," 1874.

Take my hands, and let them move
at the impulse of Thy love;
take my feet and let them be
swift and beautiful for Thee.

Take my voice, and let me sing
always, only, for my King;
take my lips and let them be
filled with messages from Thee.

Take my silver and my gold:
not a mite would I withhold;
take my intellect and use
ev'ry pow'r as Thou shalt choose.

Take my will, and make it Thine:
it shall be no longer mine;
take my heart—it is Thine own:
it shall be Thy royal throne.

Take my love, my Lord, I pour
at thy feet its treasure store;
take myself and I will be
ever, only, all for Thee.

Lord, Speak to Me[127]

Lord, speak to me that I may speak
in living echoes of Thy tone;

127 Frances R. Havergal, "Lord, Speak to Me," 1872.

as Thou hast sought, so let me seek
Thine erring children, lost and 'lone.

O strengthen me that while I stand
firm on the Rock and strong in Thee,
I may stretch out a loving hand
to wrestlers with the troubled sea.

O teach me, Lord, that I may teach
the precious things Thou dost impart;
and wing my words that they may reach
the hidden depths of many a heart.

O fill me with Thy fullness, Lord,
until my very heart o'erflow;
in kindling thought and glowing word,
Thy love to tell, Thy praise to show.

Aging and Death

There is a time for everything,
and a season for every activity under the heavens:
a time to be born and a time to die.

Ecclesiastes 3:1–2 NIV

Even to your old age and gray hairs I am he, I am he who will sustain you. I have made you and I will carry you; I will sustain you and I will rescue you.

Isaiah 46:4 NIV

Let us pray not for lighter burdens
but for stronger backs.

Anonymous

AGING

AGING WITH DIGNITY[128]

I don't want to grow old, God. I don't want any part of it. But since I have no power to stop the clock, my prayer is this: let me age with grace.

Show me the way, God. Be with me. Grant health to my body and clarity to my mind. Give me strength. Help me to overcome my vanity. Teach me to combat self-pity. Don't allow me to become set in my ways. Shield me from isolation and from loneliness.

May the love of my family and friends be my reward for all the struggles of my youth.

Let all the blessings of age emanate from me. Let wisdom flow from my mouth; let compassion flow from my heart; let acts of kindness flow from my arms; let faith flow from my soul; let joy shine forth from my eyes. Amen.

QUIET MY ANXIETY

Quiet my anxiety, heavenly Father, and remind me again of the unsearchable truth that your love for me is eternally present.

128 Martin Luther (1483–1546). Adapted.

Threescore and Ten[129]

Lord, you have been our dwelling place
through all generations.
Before the mountains were brought forth
or ever you had formed the earth and the world,
from everlasting to everlasting you are God.
You have set our iniquities before you—
our secret sins in the light of your presence.
You return man to dust and say,
"Return, O children of man!"
For a thousand years in your sight
are but as yesterday when it is passed
or as a watch in the night.
The years of our life are seventy (or eighty, if we have the strength),
yet their span is but toil and trouble.
They are soon gone, and we fly away.
So teach us to number our days, that we may get a heart of wisdom.

I Am Growing Older[130]

Lord, you know better than I myself that I am growing older and will someday be old.
Keep me from the fatal habit of thinking I must say something on every subject and on every occasion.

---

129 Psalm 90:1–12. Adapted.

130 Teresa of Ávila (1515–1582).

Release me from craving to straighten out everybody's affairs.
Make me thoughtful but not moody, helpful but not bossy.
With my vast store of wisdom, it seems a pity not to use it all. But you know, Lord, that I want a few friends at the end.
Keep my mind free from the recital of endless details; give me wings to get to the point.
Seal my lips on my aches and pains; they are increasing, and love of rehearsing them is becoming sweeter as the years go by.
I dare not ask for improved memory, but for a growing humility and a lessening cocksureness when my memory seems to clash with the memories of others.
Teach me the glorious lesson that, occasionally, I may be mistaken.
Keep me reasonably sweet, for a sour old person is one of the crowning works of the devil.
Give me the ability to see good things in unexpected places and talents in unexpected people,
and give me, O Lord, the grace to tell them so.
Amen.

Preparing for Death

Into Your Hands I Commit My Spirit[131]

O my heavenly Father,
God and Father of our Lord Jesus Christ,
God of all comfort,
I thank you for revealing to me
your dear Son, Jesus Christ,
in whom I believe,
whom I have preached and confessed,
whom I have loved and praised.

I pray, my Lord Jesus Christ,
take my soul into your hands.

Heavenly Father, I know that
although I will live in this body
and be taken from this life,
I will live with you forever,
and that no one can pluck me
out of your hands.

God so loved the world that he gave his only
begotten Son,
that whoever believes in him shall not perish,
but have eternal life.

131 Martin Luther (1483–1546).

Our God is the God of salvation,
and the Lord delivers from death.

Father, into your hands I commit my spirit.
You have redeemed me, O Lord, the God of truth.

Redeeming the Time

I know not, Lord, when my time will come
or how many years you've allotted me.
I feel keenly the weight of responsibility:
that you have called me to make the most
of what you've given me.
It is a sacred trust. Help me not to fail you.
Quicken and strengthen me,
that I may not become a lazy servant, rich fool,
ungrateful leper, Demas, Ahab, Jezebel,
Diotrephes, or Judas Iscariot.

Rather, keep my heart responsive.
Let me be like Josiah and Mary of Bethany—
focused and constantly growing in the character
of Christ.

May I not be a foolish builder,
but may I build on the solid rock of your Word.
As a steward of your trust, your image,
and your commission,
may I live out my remaining days in joyful faithfulness.

Teach me to number my days aright.
Take my life and use me.
Help me to continue to bear fruit, even in old age,
for your kingdom and to your kingdom.

I Am a Poor Wayfaring Stranger[132]

I am a poor wayfaring stranger
while traveling through this world of woe,
yet there's no sickness, toil, nor danger
in that bright world to which I go.
I'm going there to see my Father;
I'm going there no more to roam;
I'm only going over Jordan;
I'm only going over home.

I know dark clouds will gather 'round me;
I know my way is rough and steep;
but golden fields lie out before me
where God's redeemed shall ever sleep.
I'm going there to see God's children;
I know they'll meet me when I come.
I'm only going over Jordan;
I'm only going over home.

132 American folk song, "Wayfaring Stranger," *Christian Songster*, ed. Joseph Bever, 1858.

I'll soon be free from ev'ry trial,
my body sleep beneath the ground.
I'll drop the cross of self-denial
and enter on my great reward.
I'm going there to see my Savior
to sing His praise forevermore.
I'm only going over Jordan;
I'm only going over home.

Abide with Me[133]

Abide with me; fast falls the eventide;
the darkness deepens; Lord, with me abide!
When other helpers fail and comforts flee,
Help of the helpless, O abide with me!

Swift to its close ebbs out life's little day.
Earth's joys grow dim; its glories pass away.
Change and decay in all around I see;
O Thou who changest not, abide with me!

I need Thy presence ev'ry passing hour:
what but Thy grace can foil the tempter's pow'r?
Who like Thyself my guide and stay can be?
Through cloud and sunshine, O abide with me!

I fear no foe with Thee at hand to bless;
ills have no weight and tears no bitterness.

133 Henry F. Lyte, "Abide with Me," 1847.

Where is death's sting? Where, grave, thy victory?
I triumph still if Thou abide with me!

Hold Thou Thy cross before my closing eyes;
shine through the gloom, and point me to the skies;
Heav'n's morning breaks,
and earth's vain shadows flee;
in life, in death, O Lord, abide with me!

O Sacred Head (verses 7–11)[134]

My Shepherd, now receive me;
my Guardian, own me thine.
Great blessings thou didst give me,
O source of gifts divine.
Thy lips have often fed me
with words of truth and love;
thy Spirit oft hath led me
to heavenly joys above.

Here I will stand beside thee;
from thee I will not part;
O Savior, do not chide me
when breaks thy loving heart.
When soul and body languish
in death's cold, cruel grasp,

134 Bernard of Clairvaux (1090–1153), "O Sacred Head, Now Wounded," trans. Paul Gerhardt, 1656, trans. James W. Alexander, 1829, verses 7–11. Note that verses 1–4 and 6 appear in chapter 3.

then, in thy deepest anguish,
thee in mine arms I'll clasp.

The joy can never be spoken,
above all joys beside,
when in thy body broken
I thus with safety hide.
O Lord of Life, desiring
thy glory now to see,
beside thy cross expiring,
I'd breathe my soul to thee.

My Savior, be thou near me
when death is at my door;
then let thy presence cheer me;
forsake me nevermore!
When soul and body languish,
O leave me not alone,
but take away mine anguish
by virtue of thine own.

Be thou my consolation,
my shield when I must die;
remind me of thy passion
when my last hour draws nigh.
Mine eyes shall then behold thee,
upon thy cross shall dwell,
my heart by faith enfolds thee
who dieth thus dies well.

CHAPTER 10

Evening Prayer

By day the Lord directs his love,
at night his song is with me—
a prayer to the God of my life.

Psalm 42:8 niv

If your day is hemmed in with prayer,
it is less likely to come unraveled.

Cynthia Lewis

In the morning, prayer is the key that opens to us the treasures of God's mercies and blessings; in the evening, it is the key that shuts us up under His protection and safeguard.

Billy Graham (1918–2018)

The Day Is Past and Over[135]

The day is past and over;
all thanks, O Lord, to Thee!
We pray Thee that offenseless
the hours of dark may be.
O Jesus, keep us in Thy sight,
and guard us through the coming night.

The joys of day are over;
we lift our hearts to Thee
and call on Thee that sinless
the hours of dark may be.
O Jesus, make their darkness light,
and guard us through the coming night.

Lord, that in death I sleep not
and lest my foe should say,
"I have prevailed against him,"
lighten mine eyes, I pray.
O Jesus, keep me in Thy sight,
and guard me through the coming night.

Be Thou our souls' Preserver,
O God, for Thou dost know
how many are the perils
through which we have to go.

135 Anatolius of Constantinople (d. AD 458), "The Day Is Past and Over," trans. J.M. Neale, 1853.

Lord Jesus Christ, O hear our call,
and guard and save us from them all.

The toils of day are over;
we raise our hymn to Thee
and ask that free from peril
the hours of dark may be.
O Jesus, keep us in Thy sight,
and guard us through the coming night.

You Hold Me Together[136]

Father, thank you for holding me together today. I needed you, and you were there for me. Thank you for every bit of love, mercy, and grace that was shown to me, though I did not deserve it. Thank you for your faithfulness even in my suffering. To you alone be the glory. Amen.

A Good Night's Sleep[137]

Bless us with rest tonight, Lord, and a good night's sleep. Forgive us for the things we did today that did not honor you. Thank you for loving us so much, even though you know us through and through. We need your help every day, and we thank you for the

136 Topher Haddox, "7 Quick Inspirational Prayers to Help You throughout Your Day," Crosswalk, July 12, 2019, crosswalk.com.

137 Rebecca Barlow Jordan, "40 Good Night Prayers for Peaceful Rest in the Evening," Crosswalk, July 5, 2024, crosswalk.com. Adapted.

strength you give. Bless our family and our home, and keep us safe through the night. May your angels guard us and watch over us.

You lead us and guard us like a shepherd. You know our names, and you make us feel special and loved. When we hurt, you help us feel better. Thank you, Jesus, for your good care and for putting others in our lives to help us. Thank you for the Bible—for teaching us how to live life.

Help us to obey you and love you more and more. When we awake in the morning, put a smile on our face and your purpose in our hearts, and make us ready to start a new day. We love you, Lord. Amen.

Sleep in Peace[138]

O Eternal God and King of all creation, who has granted me to arrive at this hour, forgive me the sins that I have committed today in thought, word, and deed. And cleanse, O Lord, my humble soul from all defilement of flesh and spirit. And grant me, O Lord, to pass the sleep of this night in peace, that when I rise from my bed, I may please your most holy name all the days of my life and conquer my flesh and the fleshless foes that war against me. And deliver me, O Lord, from vain and frivolous thoughts and from evil desires that defile me. For yours is the kingdom,

138 Macarius of Egypt (c. AD 300–391).

the power, and the glory of the Father, Son, and Holy Spirit, now and ever and to the ages of ages. Amen.

Deep Spiritual Rest[139]

Heavenly Father, who gives rest to his children, will you wash over me a peace that passes all understanding as I lie down to sleep tonight? I ask that you would ease the load of the burdens I am carrying. My desire is to be an effective parent, spouse, and friend, and I know my attitude, energy level, and spiritual life will not be sufficient to do this if I don't have the deep spiritual rest you long to give me. Be merciful, O Lord, and give sweet sleep to your child. In Jesus' name. Amen.

Unburdening the Heart[140]

Father, I have worked hard today, and I am tired. Thank you for giving me a chance to make use of the gifts you gave me, for my own good and for the good of others.

Thank you for making me work hard today and enabling me to find fulfillment in what I have accomplished. Yet at times today, selfishness, pride, and haughtiness took hold of me. In anger and impatience, I lost my temper, and I may have

139 Lysa TerKeurst, "40 Good Night Prayers for Peaceful Rest in the Evening," Crosswalk, July 5, 2024, crosswalk.com. Adapted.

140 "Evening II," *Presence*, 132–33. Adapted.

wounded the feelings of others. Curses, lies, and the dishonesty of those who surrounded me today have also burdened my heart.

So I pray to you now, dear Father, that you would cleanse and unburden my heart of this day's anxieties and tensions. After this long and hard day, let peace settle on me so that I may rest in your love tonight. Amen.

For a Young Child[141]

Now I lay me down to sleep;
I pray the Lord my soul to keep.
May angels watch me through the night
and keep me safe till morning's light.

A Quiet Mind[142]

And now, O God, give me a quiet mind as I lie down to rest. Dwell in my thoughts until sleep overtakes me. Let me rejoice in the knowledge that, whether awake or asleep, I am with Thee. Let me not be fretted by any anxiety over the lesser interests of life. Let no troubled dreams disturb me so that I may

---

141 Debbie Trafton O'Neal and Nancy Munger, *Now I Lay Me Down to Sleep: Action Prayers, Poems, and Songs for Bedtime* (Augsburg Fortress, 1994), 6. Adapted.

142 John Baillie, *A Diary of Private Prayer* (Charles Scribner's Sons, 1949), 55.

awake refreshed and ready for the tasks of another day. And to Thy name be all the glory. Amen.

The Close of Day[143]

O Lord my God, I thank you that you have brought this day to a close.
I thank you that you have given me peace in body and in soul. Your hand has been over me and has protected and preserved me.
Forgive my puny faith and the ill that I have done this day, and help me to forgive all who have wronged me.
Grant me a quiet night's sleep beneath your tender care and defend me from all the temptations of darkness.
Into your hands I commend my loved ones and all who dwell in this house. I commend to you my body and soul.
O Lord God, your holy name be praised.

The Evening Prayer[144]

Merciful Lord,
let the evening prayer of your church
come before you.
May we do your work faithfully;

143 Dietrich Bonhoeffer (1906–1945).

144 From the Breviary, Evening Prayer for Wednesday in the 28th Week of Ordinary Time, ibreviary.com.

free us from sin and make us secure in your love.
We ask this through our Lord Jesus Christ, your Son,
who lives and reigns with you and the Holy Spirit,
one God, forever and ever. Amen.

An Evening Hymn[145]

All praise to Thee, my God, this night
for all the blessings of the light!
Keep me, O keep me, King of kings,
beneath Thine own almighty wings.

Forgive me, Lord, for Thy dear Son,
the ill that I this day have done
that with the world, myself, and Thee,
I, ere I sleep, at peace may be.

Teach me to live that I may dread
the grave as little as my bed.
Teach me to die so that I may
rise glorious at the judgment day.

O may my soul on Thee repose
and with sweet sleep mine eyelids close—
sleep that may me more vigorous make
to serve my God when I awake.

When in the night I sleepless lie,
my soul with heavenly thoughts supply;

145 Thomas Ken, "An Evening Hymn," 1709.

let no ill dreams disturb my rest—
no powers of darkness me molest.

O when shall I, in endless day,
forever chase dark sleep away
and hymns divine with angels sing,
"All praise to thee, eternal King"?

Praise God, from Whom all blessings flow;
praise Him, all creatures here below;
praise Him above, ye heavenly host;
praise Father, Son, and Holy Ghost.

It Is Well with My Soul[146]

When peace, like a river, attendeth my way,
when sorrows like sea billows roll,
whatever my lot, Thou has taught me to say,
"It is well, it is well with my soul."

Though Satan should buffet,
though trials should come,
let this blest assurance control:
that Christ has regarded my helpless estate
and hath shed His own blood for my soul.

146 Horatio G. Spafford, "When Peace, Like a River," 1873.

My sin, O the bliss of this glorious thought—
my sin, not in part, but the whole,
is nailed to the cross, and I bear it no more:
praise the Lord, praise the Lord, O my soul!

For me, be it Christ—be it Christ hence to live;
if dark hours about me shall roll,
no pang shall be mine, for in death as in life
Thou wilt whisper Thy peace to my soul.

But Lord, 'tis for Thee, for Thy coming we wait:
the sky, not the grave, is our goal.
O, trump of the angel! O, voice of the Lord!
Blessed hope—blessed rest of my soul!

And Lord, haste the day when the faith shall be sight,
the clouds be rolled back as a scroll.
The trump shall resound,
and the Lord shall descend;
Even so, it is well with my soul.

CHAPTER 11

Intercession

I urge that supplications, prayers, intercessions, and thanksgivings be made for all people, for kings and all who are in high positions, that we may lead a peaceful and quiet life, godly and dignified in every way.

1 Timothy 2:1–2 ESV

As for me, far be it from me that I should sin against the Lord by failing to pray for you.

1 Samuel 12:23 NIV

Worship and intercession must go together; the one is impossible without the other. Intercession means that we rouse ourselves up to get the mind of Christ about the one for whom we pray.

Oswald Chambers (1874–1917)

Men may spurn our appeals, reject our message, oppose our arguments, despise our persons, but they are helpless against our prayers.

J. Sidlow Baxter (1903–1999)

The Global Body of Christ

Lord, your people around the globe need you now more than ever. We are confronted with so much evil: violence, racism, consumerism, atheism, perversion, and narcissism.

We turn to you for strength and guidance. Yet we are not fully devoted to studying your Word. Help us to take Scripture seriously.

We long for your holiness. Yet we are beset with sin and struggles and often fail to love our brothers and sisters in Christ—especially those far away or from different backgrounds and cultures. Instill in us the fear of God.

We place so much value on being right and are often dismissive of others when their perspectives differ. Our lack of humility is obvious to the watching world. We are divided and divisive—so sectarian that often we fail to recognize the image of Christ in others, writing them off as nonbelievers even when the Spirit burns hot in their lives. Root out our sectarianism. Help us to listen. Open our eyes.

Father, we know that Jesus died for the church. Bless the church universal and keep her faithful to the mission.

A Prayer for the Church[147]

We ask that you send the Holy Spirit as a holy offering to the holy church. As we assemble, give to all the saints the fullness of the Holy Spirit for the confirmation of true faith so that we may praise and glorify you through your Son, Jesus Christ, through whom glory and honor to the Father and the Son with the Holy Spirit in your holy church are yours now and forever. Amen.

Christians in Need[148]

We ask you, Master, be our helper and defender. Rescue those of our number in distress, raise up the fallen, assist the needy, heal the sick, turn back those of your people who stray, feed the hungry, release our captives, revive the weak, and encourage those who lose heart. Let all the nations realize that you are the only God, that Jesus Christ is your Child, and that we are your people and the sheep of your pasture.

---

147 Hippolytus of Rome (c. AD 170–235).

148 Clement of Rome (c. AD 35–99).

The Local Body of Christ

I ask your blessings on my local church. Help us to build family. Help us to reach out to our community. Help us to focus and not become distracted by the things of the world—or even by too many programs in the church.

I promise to be invested emotionally in the church and to do my part to meet the financial needs of the congregation.

Guide our leaders. Help them to be men and women of your Word and to lead us with integrity, faith, gentleness, and respect. Help us to be supportive of them and patient even when things move slower than we desire and we feel frustrated.

Help us to understand that we are all in Christian ministry, a priesthood of believers and a holy nation. Bless the church of Christ.

Christian Missionaries

Today I want to remember those who have left the security of their country to take the message where Christ is not known.

I pray you will keep them safe, Lord. Give them great vision for what they can accomplish by your boundless power. Help them to be fearless.

I promise to support missionaries even if funding runs out. For I know that it is your will that your Word cover the earth and that all have an opportunity to hear the good news.

A Loved One in Need of Faith

Lord, you know how much I care about ____________. As we spend time together in the Scriptures, please bring my friend to a saving faith. Help them not to resist the sobering implications of the biblical message. Give them the faith and the strength to make you their Lord. You know how deeply I long for ____________ to become a true disciple of Christ. Be with them and be with me, through the power of Jesus Christ.

The Sick

Someone I care about deeply is sick. I ask that, if it is your will, you restore them to health. Whether through medicine or through prayer alone, please heal them. I am not requesting the blessings of long life or perfect health; I am only asking that your will be done. Your healing power is beyond measure. Glorify your name, O Lord.

For Healing[149]

Watch, O Lord, with those who
cannot sleep or who weep tonight.
Tend your sick ones.
Rest your weary ones.
Bless your dying ones.
Soothe your suffering ones.
Pity your afflicted ones.
Shield your joyous ones.
Amen.

Our Marriage[150]

O eternal and gracious Father, you have set marriage apart as a holy mystery, a representation of the union of Christ with his church. Please let the Holy Spirit guide me as a spouse that it may not become a sin to me, and do not let the liberties that you have righteously given by holy Jesus become an occasion of licentiousness for my own weakness and sensuality.

Let me in all experiences and circumstances be serious about my service for you. Let me be affectionate and loving to my spouse; a guide and good example for my family; and in all quietness, sobriety, prudence, and peace, a follower of those

149 Augustine of Hippo (AD 354–430).
150 Jeremy Taylor (1613–1667). Adapted.

holy couples who have served you with godliness and good testimony.

Please let the blessings of the eternal God, the blessings of the right hand and of the left, be upon the body and soul of your servant and my spouse, and let those blessings remain until we have come to the end of a holy and happy life. Please grant that both of us may live forever in the embrace of the holy and eternal Jesus, our Lord and Savior. Amen.

My Wife

Lord, I thank you for giving me my life partner. She is precious to me and to many others. Help me to love, cherish, and support her. Help me to make her feel special. Help me to see my own faults before I see hers. Help me to be patient with her just as she is patient with me. Even when it is hard to feel affectionate or when our marriage suffers strain, may I never use hurtful words or sarcasm. May I honor and respect her always—spiritually, physically, emotionally, and sexually.

Continue to convict me, O God, of the vital importance of keeping all my wedding vows. I have made a sacred promise. May I be a man of integrity. Preserve our marriage till death parts us. Amen.

My Husband

Lord, I thank you for giving me my life partner. He is precious to me and to many others. Help me to love, cherish, and support him. Help me make him feel special. Help me to see my own faults before I see his. Help me to be patient with him just as he is patient with me. Even when it is hard to feel affectionate or when our marriage suffers strain, may I never use hurtful words or sarcasm. May I honor and respect him always—spiritually, emotionally, physically, and sexually.

Continue to convict me, O God, of the vital importance of keeping my wedding vows. May I be a woman of integrity. Preserve our marriage till death parts us. Amen.

My Children

Heavenly Father, bless my children. They are a gift from you, and being a parent is a privilege. I've tried hard to do what is right, yet I have still fallen short in many ways. Help me to be a better parent.

May I provide my children with the affection and guidance they need and crave. May I be an example of a spiritual parent to them, righteous and always growing. As they mature, help me to gradually let go, not putting unhealthy pressure on them. And may I show full respect to my adult children. Amen.

Old Gallican Rite[151]

Have mercy, O Lord, on all those whom you have associated with us in the bonds of friendship and family. Grant that they, with us, may be so perfectly conformed to your holy will that, being cleansed from all sin, we may be found worthy, by the inspiration of your love, to participate together in the blessedness of your heavenly kingdom through Jesus Christ our Lord. Amen.

My Parents

You are my heavenly Father, and you know I am eternally grateful to be a beloved member of your family. I'm also grateful for my earthly family. I'm striving to love and honor my parents, knowing your clear command to honor father and mother. I know they have sacrificed much for me.

Help me to imitate the good in them: their generosity, wisdom, and strength of character. May I also be graciously discerning about any generational baggage they have received from their parents. May I not blame my parents for things that are my own

151 Old Gallican Rite, "10 Prayers from History to Pray for Your Loved Ones," Crossway, crossway.org.

responsibility. May I always seek to honor them in conversation, in caring for their needs, and in memory. Amen.

My Friends

Heavenly Father, although we cherish above all our relationship with you, we also deeply appreciate the companionship of our friends. They are more important than all that we could ever achieve, earn, or acquire.

Today I bring ___________ before you. Through our relationship, please bring them comfort, confidence, and encouragement. Bring them closer to you.

May I be a friend to all who need me. Give me vision to realize how you may intend to use me to make a difference in their lives.

Help me to form new friendships with people I will cherish and with whom I will form lifelong bonds. Thank you for this most precious gift. Amen.

Enemies

Dear Lord, I unfortunately have an enemy. I am struggling not to hate, curse, and disdain them. I truly desire to love, bless, and respect them. Give me the right heart: a heart to serve, not to abuse. Remove far from me even the beginning of a spirit of revenge. May I have no seed of desire to hurt them by any means, illegal or even legal. My greatest hope is that my enemy may someday become a friend. But if that is not possible, I still promise to live at peace with them as far as it depends on me.

Jesus died for his enemies. Increase in me the love of Christ and my willingness to suffer, for I know that suffering is part of love.

Governmental Authorities

At this time I remember those who rule over us in positions of governmental authority. I appreciate that governance is essential for the good of society. Help our leaders to govern in peace, especially by fostering conditions favoring the more rapid spread of the good news.

Please, Lord, strengthen me to be a good and obedient citizen who is willing to comply with any law that does not violate your holy Word.

May I never seek to undermine law and order through criminal acts, cheating on taxes, slandering officials, or negative speech. In my comments, written words, social media posts, and general attitude, help me to exude respect and grace. Even if the authorities fall woefully short of your righteous standards, cultivate in me a genuine love for them.

Where Faith Is Outlawed

I dwell in a nation where living out my faith is illegal. Give me courage not to fear prison, torture, or death. Enable me to love my enemies, conduct myself with grace, and always remember the sufferings of our Lord.

For Persecuted Christians[152]

Dear Heavenly Father,

Thank you for our persecuted Christian brothers and sisters who faithfully stand as witnesses of Your grace no matter the cost. When they are beaten and delivered to courts, may they gain confidence through Your presence in all situations.

As they stand before any opponent—whether family members, former friends, or government authorities—replace their anxiety with peace, love, and faith.

When they face slander, allegations, and legal charges, may they speak boldly, lovingly, and truthfully with wisdom. Give our bold and faithful persecuted brothers and sisters courage and endurance as they recall Jesus' promise that His followers would face persecution.

Thank you for their sacrifice and faithfulness. We join them in joyful praise to the name above all names: Jesus. Amen.

---

152 *Voice of the Martyrs*, January 2021.

A Prayer for the People of God[153]

Dear Lord, remember this city where your people dwell and every other city and country with your faithful followers in them.

O Lord, remember all who sail and those who travel by land, those who are sick or who are close to death, and those who are captives in need of freedom.

Remember, O Lord, those who display good fruit—those who cultivate the soil of your holy church and do not neglect the poor. Grant that, in unity of voice and heart, we may glorify and praise your great and majestic name—Father, Son, and Holy Spirit—both now and forevermore. Amen.

Immortal, Invisible, God Only Wise[154]

Immortal, invisible, God only wise,
in light inaccessible hid from our eyes,
most blessed, most glorious, the Ancient of Days,
almighty, victorious, Thy great name we praise.

Unresting, unhasting, and silent as light,
nor wanting nor wasting, Thou rulest in might:

153 The Byzantine Liturgy of Chrysostom, fifth century AD.

154 Walter Chalmers Smith, "Immortal, Invisible, God Only Wise," 1867.

Thy justice like mountains high-soaring above,
Thy clouds which are fountains of goodness and love.

To all life Thou givest, to both great and small.
In all life Thou livest—the true life of all.
Thy wisdom so boundless, Thy mercy so free,
eternal Thy goodness, for naught changeth Thee.

Great Father of glory, pure Father of light,
Thine angels attend Thee, all veiling their sight.
All laud we would render; O help us to see
'tis only the splendor of light hideth Thee.

Glory, Laud, and Honor[155]

All glory, laud, and honor
to Thee, Redeemer, King!
To Whom the lips of children
may sweet Hosannas ring.
Thou art the King of Israel,
Thou David's royal Son,
Who in the Lord's name comest,
the King and Blessed One.

The company of angels
is praising Thee on high,
and mortal men and all things
created make reply.

155 Theodulf of Orléans (c. AD 750–821), "All Glory, Laud, and Honor," trans. John Mason Neale, 1854. Adapted.

The people of the Hebrews
with palms before Thee went;
our praise and prayers and anthems
before Thee we present.

To Thee before Thy Passion
they sang their hymns of praise;
to Thee now high exalted
our melody we raise.
Thou didst accept their praises;
accept the praise we bring,
Who in all good delightest,
Thou good and gracious King.

Lord, I Come before Thee Now[156]

Lord, I come before Thee now;
at Thy feet I humbly bow.
O do not my suit disdain.
Shall I seek Thee, Lord, in vain?

Lord, on Thee my soul depends;
in compassion now descend.
Fill my heart with Thy rich grace;
tune my lips to sing Thy praise.

In Thine own appointed way,
now I seek Thee; here I stay.

156 William Hammond, "Opening Worship," 1745. Adapted.

Lord, I know not how to go
till a blessing Thou bestow.

Grant that all may seek and find
Thee a God supremely kind.
Heal the sick, the captive free;
let us all rejoice in Thee.

Special Needs and Occasions

Pray in the Spirit on all occasions
with all kinds of prayers and requests.

Ephesians 6:18 NIV

Prayer moves the arm which moves the world
and brings salvation down.

James Montgomery (1771–1854)

Serenity[157]

God, grant me the serenity
to accept the things I cannot change,
the courage to change the things I can,

157 The Alcoholics Anonymous version of the Serenity Prayer is an abbreviation of this original, famous prayer by Reinhold Niebuhr (1892–1971). Adapted.

and the wisdom to know the difference.
Living one day at a time,
enjoying one moment at a time,
accepting hardship as a pathway to peace,
taking (as Jesus did)
this sinful world as it is,
not as I would have it,
trusting that You will make all things right
if I surrender to Your will
so that I may be reasonably happy in this life
and supremely happy with You forever in the next.
Amen.

Long Journey

I am about to embark on a long trip, and I request your help. You guided the children of Israel out of Egypt and into the promised land. You brought Ezra all the way from Babylon to Jerusalem. Joseph and Mary walked from Nazareth to Judea. The wise men traveled from Persia to Bethlehem. You brought Paul all the way to Rome. These journeys were not easy for the travelers, yet you sustained them. I know, then, that you have the power to safeguard me on my trip.

Keep me safe every step of the way. Help me to be alert. Protect me from getting lost, from stormy weather, and from those who might wish to hurt or exploit me. Help me to remember that I am yours, and that my behavior away from home ought to be as righteous as my behavior when I am at home.

Let me be aware of you every step of the way, Lord, and return me safely.

Birthday

By your grace, Lord, I have lived another year. Looking back, I realize that you have been with me, empowering me to reach goals although still I have fallen short. I realize also that my goals are not necessarily your goals for me. Help me in this next year to strive harder to be like Christ—to keep growing in holiness, maturity, and wisdom.

Anniversary

Today, on our wedding anniversary, I thank you for my spouse. What a privilege it is to have one. There have been good times and hard times, and we have stuck together through thick and thin. May we respect, care for, and adore one another for many years to come.

Celibacy

I give thanks to you, Lord, for the gift of singleness, which you have given me. Like Paul, Anna, and Jesus, I am content to remain unmarried, and your Word assures us that this is truly a gift. My life is simpler, less distracted, and more streamlined as I serve you, God.

Yet sometimes it's hard not to feel discouraged when society pressures singles to find partners, and sometimes it hurts when fellow Christians tease me. Help me to stay the course.

Social Justice

Prophetic Cry[158]

With what shall I come before the Lord and bow down before the exalted God?
Shall I come before him with burnt offerings or calves a year old?
Will the Lord be pleased with thousands of rams or ten thousand rivers of olive oil?
Shall I offer my firstborn for my transgression?
He has shown me, a mere mortal, what is good.
And what does the Lord require of me?
He calls me to act justly and to love mercy and to walk humbly with my God.
And when I accept this truth and live this way,
let justice roll on like a river
and righteousness like a never-failing stream.

158 Micah 6:6–8 and Amos 5:24. Adapted.

Reversal[159]

I rejoice in your salvation.
There is none holy like the Lord
for there is none besides you;
there is no rock like our God.
The Lord is a God of knowledge,
and by him actions are weighed.
The bows of the mighty are broken,
but the feeble bind on strength.
The Lord raises up the poor from the dust;
he lifts the needy from the ash heap
to make them sit with princes and
inherit a seat of honor.
He will guard the feet of his faithful ones,
but the wicked shall be cut off in darkness,
for not by might shall a man prevail.
The adversaries of the Lord shall be broken to pieces;
against them he will thunder in heaven.
The Lord will judge the ends of the earth.

The Serpent and the Dove[160]

Dear Lord, you have sent me into this world to preach your Word. So often the problems of the world seem so complex and intricate that your Word strikes me as

159 Hannah's prayer in 1 Samuel 2:1–10. Adapted.

160 Henri Nouwen, *The HarperCollins Book of Prayers: A Treasury of Prayers through the Ages,* ed. Robert Van de Weyer (Castle Books, 1997), 273.

embarrassingly simple. Many times I feel tongue-tied in the company of people who are dealing with the world's social and economic problems.

But you, O Lord, said, "Be clever as serpents and innocent as doves." Let me retain innocence and simplicity in the midst of this complex world. I realize that I have to be informed, that I have to study the many aspects of the problems facing the world, and that I have to try as well as possible to understand the dynamics of our contemporary society. But what really counts is that all this information, knowledge, and insight allows me to speak more clearly and unambiguously your truthful Word.

Do not allow evil powers to seduce me with the complexities of the world's problems, but give me the strength to think clearly, speak freely, and act boldly in your service. Give me the courage to show the dove in a world so full of serpents.

Death

A dear friend has died. I feel shock, grief, and sadness, yet I know this is not the end. Mortal life is followed by the afterlife. Lord, you speak to us of these things in your Word. If you hadn't, we would have no hope, grieving like the rest of humankind, like those who do not know you.

I remember the good things. Thank you for the time we shared. Bring comfort to the family and to the mourners.

Godly men mourned for Stephen and buried him. When my friend is buried, I will mourn, and I will never forget them. And as my friend was a sincere Christian, I look forward to our reunion in paradise.

Anniversary of a Death

It's that day again—the day we lost ____________. I miss them terribly. Through your omniscience and through the cross, Jesus, you know the pain of death and can comfort the grieving. I'm hurting, and I seek your heavenly support. Help me to make it through this process. I know I'll never stop missing ______________, but by your grace I can make the necessary adjustments so that their memory is honored while my life goes on. I am overwhelmed with grief and profound sadness. Be with me, Lord.

Natural Disaster[161]

We are devastated, Lord God. Disaster has struck. Many have lost their homes or lives. Scientists have explained how fires and storms and earthquakes are

---

161 See Psalm 46:1–3, 10. Debbie McDaniel, "40 Good Night Prayers for Peaceful Rest in the Evening," Crosswalk, July 5, 2024, crosswalk.com.

part of the lifecycle of the world. Without them we would not be here. All the same, we are devastated. You are our refuge and strength; you are a present help in time of trouble.

Therefore we will not fear, though the earth gives way, though mountains be moved into the heart of the sea, though its waters roar and foam, and though the mountains tremble at its swelling. Help us to be still and know that you are God.

In Times of War

O Lord, our nation is at war. Many people will lose their lives—not only soldiers but also innocent women and children. Widows and orphans will proliferate. Populations will be displaced. Hatred will intensify. Vengeance will be sworn. The toll will be heavy on both sides.

Prevent me from being swept up into the rhetoric and the violence. You taught us to love our enemies. I do not hate the enemy. The causes for which armies fight are not ultimate. Territory, resources, power, wealth—these will not endure. They are not eternal. All that counts is a relationship with you. You taught us to bless our enemies and not to curse them. You taught us to love our enemies—to care for them, feed them, and show compassion. Help me also to forgive my own countrymen who take my opposition to violence as hatred for my country. It isn't true; I love my country. Please show me the best way to serve your purposes in this time of war.

Prayer for Peace[162]

Lord Jesus, we come to you in our need. Create in us an awareness of the massive forces of conflict and evil that threaten our world today. Grant us a sense of urgency to activate the forces of goodness, justice, love, and peace.

Where there is armed conflict, let us stretch out our arms to our brothers and sisters. Where there is abundance, let there be simple lifestyles and sharing. Where there is poverty, let there be dignified living and loving sacrifice to share with all those in need. Where there is selfish ambition, let there be humble service. Where there is injustice, let there be atonement. Where there is despair, let there be hope in the good news. Where there are wounds of division, let there be unity and wholeness.

Help us to be committed to the building of your kingdom: not seeking to be cared for, but to care; not expecting to be served, but to place ourselves in the

162 "EDSA Prayer for Peace," *Peace by Peace,* March–April 2007, misyononline.info-aid.net.

service of others; and not aspiring to be materially secure, but to place our security in your love.

Conform us to your Spirit, for it is only in loving imitation of you, Lord, that we discover the healing springs of life that will bring about new birth on the earth and hope for the world. Amen.

Spiritual Leadership

Leadership is a privilege, and great good can come from leadership that is truly holy.
Yet you warn us not to lord it over others.
May I seek to serve and not to control.
May I truly care for those to whom I minister, leading them gently and treating them as I myself would want to be led.
May I lead by example and not by command.
May I lead by relationship and not by authority.
May I speak the truth in love.
In my leadership, help me to observe your mandate to love everybody, serve the needy, and teach others to obey your commands.
Thank you for Jesus, who served as the perfect example.
When I'm unsure how to handle a situation, may I look to him, following his lead.

Before Sunday Service[163]

Praise the Lord, O my soul;
praise the Lord.
Let gladness come:
smiles and laughter
at the beauty and bounty
which surround me.
It is supplied by your hand—
freely given so that I can give
bountifully to others,
spreading smiles and laughter.
Eye to eye, let me see
each person and their needs.
Let me see you
working in their lives.
Each of us is giving;
each of us is receiving.
The sweet fellowship of the Spirit
lives in us all.

Financial Wisdom

Dear Lord, help me to be financially responsible: to be organized, plan well, pay the bills on time, and realize that you have made me a steward of what is not mine to begin with. Every good gift I've received comes from you.

---

163 Lisa Sawhill (Athens, Georgia), personal prayer, 2020.

Help me to save, share, and spend wisely. Help me save for the future, lest I be a burden on others. Help me share with the needy and with the church. Help me to spend prudently, not going into debt for things I don't really need.

Money is dangerous and, like power, easily corrupts the soul. Protect me from the corrosive effects of materialism. May I not be motivated by envy to acquire and flaunt wealth. May I live modestly, valuing only what is truly valuable. And most of all, may I be grateful for what I have and not grumpy over what I do not have. Help me to learn Paul's secret of contentment in any situation, whether I have much or little.

Clearly, Dearly, Nearly[164]

Thanks be to you, my Lord Jesus Christ,
for all the benefits you have won for me
and for all the pains and insults you have
borne for me.
O most merciful Redeemer, friend, and brother,
may I know you more clearly,
love you more dearly,
and follow you more nearly,
forever and ever.

164 Richard of Chichester (1197–1253). Adapted.

On the Word of God[165]

Grant, Almighty God, that as you shine on us by your Word, we may not be blind at midnight nor willfully seek darkness and thus lull our minds asleep. But may we be roused daily by your words, and may we stir up ourselves more and more to fear your name and thus present ourselves and all our pursuits as a sacrifice to you, that you may peaceably rule and perpetually dwell in us until you gather us to your celestial habitation, where there is reserved for us eternal rest and glory through Jesus Christ our Lord. Amen.

Joyful, Joyful, We Adore Thee[166]

Joyful, joyful, we adore Thee,
God of glory, Lord of love;
hearts unfold like flow'rs before Thee,
op'ning to the sun above.
Melt the clouds of sin and sadness;
drive the dark of doubt away;
Giver of immortal gladness,
fill us with the light of day.

165 John Calvin (1509–1564).

166 Henry van Dyke, "Joyful, Joyful, We Adore Thee," 1907.

All Thy works with joy surround Thee;
earth and heav'n reflect Thy rays;
stars and angels sing around Thee,
center of unbroken praise.
Field and forest, vale and mountain,
flow'ry meadow, flashing sea,
chanting bird, and flowing fountain
call us to rejoice in Thee.

Thou art giving and forgiving,
ever blessing, ever blest,
well-spring of the joy of living,
ocean-depth of happy rest.
Thou our Father, Christ our brother—
all who live in love are Thine.
Teach us how to love each other;
lift us to the joy divine.

Mortals join the mighty chorus
which the morning stars began;
God's own love is reigning o'er us
brother-love binds man to man.
Ever singing, march we onward,
victors in the midst of strife;
joyful music lifts us sunward
in the triumph song of life.

O Master, Let Me Walk with Thee[167]

O Master, let me walk with Thee
in lowly depths of service free.
Tell me Thy secret; help me bear
the strain of toil, the fret of care.

Help me the slow of heart to move
by some clear, winning word of love.
Teach me the wayward feet to stay
and guide them in the homeward way.

In hope that sends a shining ray
far down the future's broad'ning way.
In peace that only Thou canst give,
with Thee, O Master, let me live.

167 Washington Gladden, "O Master, Let Me Walk with Thee," 1879.

Pray without Ceasing

Be joyful in hope, patient in affliction,
faithful in prayer.

Romans 12:12 NIV

Work, work, from morning until late at night. In fact, I have so much to do that I shall have to spend the first three hours in prayer!

Martin Luther (1483–1546)

Little of the Word with little prayer is death to the spiritual life. Much of the Word with little prayer gives a sickly life. Much prayer with little of the Word gives more life, but without steadfastness. A full measure of the Word and prayer each day gives healthy and powerful life.

Andrew Murray (1828–1917)

When words fail us, when we seek structure for our thoughts, or when we simply don't know what to say, hopefully *Amen and Amen* will supply the words.

May this little book, for years to come, prove to be a blessing in our lives and in our ministry as followers of Christ. As the apostle Paul urged, let us "pray without ceasing" (1 Thessalonians 5:17 ESV).

The Examen[168,169]

1. **Give thanks.**
   Spend a few moments in gratitude for the gifts and blessings of the day.

2. **Ask for light.**
   As you review the day, ask God to show where he has been at work and present through events, people, and places.

3. **Review the day.**
   Review the moments of the day, noticing how you have reacted to these events, people, and places.[170]

---

168 These five introspective prompts originate from the spiritual exercises of Ignatius of Loyola (1491–1556).

169 "How to Do the Examen," Pray As You Go, August 8, 2022, pray-as-you-go.org.

170 Ignatius spoke of these reactions in terms of consolation and desolation. *Consolation* directs our focus outside and beyond ourselves, lifts our hearts so that we can see the joys and sorrows of others, bonds us more closely to our human community, generates new inspiration and ideas, restores balance and refreshes our inner

4. **Seek forgiveness.**

   Ask God's forgiveness for the times when you have acted, spoken, or thought contrary to his grace and calling for you.

5. **Resolve to change.**

   Decide what in your behavior or attitude you will try to improve tomorrow.

O Lord, Our Lord[171]

O Lord, our Lord, how excellent thy name—
how excellent is Thy name in all the earth!
Thou have set Thy glory above the heavens!
We'll praise Thy holy name forever, evermore.

We'll praise and magnify
Thy name forevermore.
We'll laud and magnify
Thy holy name forevermore.

---

vision, shows us where God is active in our lives and in what directions he is leading us, and releases new energy in us.

Desolation turns us in on ourselves. It drives us down the spiral into our own negative feelings, cuts us off from community, makes us want to give up on the things that used to be important to us, takes over our whole consciousness and crowds out long-term vision, covers up all our landmarks (the signs of our journey with God so far), and drains us of energy. (Vinita Hampton Wright, "Consolation and Desolation," ignatianspirituality.com.)

171 Horatio Palmer, "O Lord, Our Lord," 1874. Adapted.

ACKNOWLEDGMENTS

I owe a debt to the many people who helped build the collection of prayers and hymns that appear in *Amen and Amen.* Let me begin by thanking BroadStreet Publishing for their interest and support, and in particular, my editor, Nina Rose, for her sharp eye, patience, and many useful suggestions.

I am deeply grateful for submissions from Bill Gaultiere ("The Apprentice Prayer" in chapter 9); J. Tyrone Marcus ("Divine Majesty" in chapter 3); Kim Pullen ("Trust" in chapter 4); Lisa Sawhill ("In This Lonely Place" in chapter 5, "Disappointment" in chapter 5, "The Giver" in chapter 7, and "Before Sunday Service" in chapter 12); and Ron Sawhill ("Father Hear My Prayer" in chapter 3 and "Thanks, Praise, and Glory" in chapter 8).

Shelley FitzGibbon, Jeff Hickman, Patti Hunter, Steve Jacoby, Jim Long, Brett Kreider, Tyrone Marcus, Dave Pocta, Kim Pullen, Lisa and Ron Sawhill, Joe Sciortino, and Elizabeth Thompson made many helpful suggestions. I am thankful for each of them.

Thanks are also due to my longtime friend and publisher Toney Mulhollan, who produced *Amen: Collected Prayers and Hymns for the Journey* (2022). Our last forty years together have been quite an adventure! The present volume, *Amen and Amen,* is a revised version of *Amen,* which itself was inspired by *Presence: Prayers for Busy People* (St Pauls Publications, 1991).

Finally, I am most appreciative of my wife, Vicki, for her great ideas and constant support. It is an honor to share with her in our common ministry.

ABOUT THE AUTHOR

Douglas Jacoby is an international Bible teacher, professor, author, podcaster, apologist, speaker, and tour guide of the biblical world. He holds degrees from Drew, Harvard, and Duke Universities. He and his wife, Vicki, reside in Britain. Learn more about his ministry at www.DouglasJacoby.com.